I0468336

Survive Police Contact

Table of Contents

Self Published Authors Network

Ordering information

Quantity Sales. Special discounts are available in quantity purchases by corporations, associations, networking groups. For details contact www.SelfPublishedAuthorsNetwork the address above

Individual Sales-

Louis Frederick Lfrederick09@yahoo.com

817-899-1537

www.selfpublishingnetwork.com

Includes biographical references and index

Dedication

This book dedicated to my loving wife Joyce my queen, and to my father Bishop L. C. Frederick Sr. who taught me what true bravery was, and to the good officers forced into silence, as well as the good citizens forced into submission.

Foreword:

In a society as diversely populated as ours there will always be cultural clashes, and miscues. There will also be abuses, and tragedies. Many times the diversities of our culture will lead to confrontations. Frequently these confrontations are plastered all over the internet, and the news media. Bad news sells, and hot emotions are super conductors for bad news. I believe that most encounters with law enforcement are routine but the current perception for most Americans is the opposite. I have observed that from a psychological perspective perception is reality. We can all agree that even one occurrence is one occurrence too many.

Within the pages of this book I will recall for you actual stories of citizens, and police encounters, and break down the actions of both parties while evaluating the outcomes of the encounters.

My ultimate goal is for you to survive. If we as a nation want to move forward into a better America it is paramount that we learn from our painful past, while continuing to work together for a right, and noble future. A future that our children, and grandchildren deserve.

The commitment of each citizen of these United States as well as each sworn, and unsworn member of the law enforcement community will be necessary for the needless eradication of American citizens to come to an end. That being said let me make it perfectly clear "It is not my intention that everyone survives the shift in law enforcement tactics, and policies that in this season seem to be thrust upon us. Some people on both sides will need to go. And I bear no remorse for their fates. This book will not be an effort to justify or explain away racist, abusive, criminal, or leech like behavior of so called leaders on either side of the thin blue line. It will be informative and thought provoking, maybe even galvanizing on some points but in either case it will serve as a tool to help us all survive police contact.

Louis Frederick

VEHICLE TRAFFIC STOPS

Vehicle traffic stops are a necessary, and important tool; for law enforcement. They are also the second most dangerous function of law enforcement. The primary duty of the police officer is to keep us safe by responding to calls from the general populace for help, as well as provide some levels of proactive policing which serve as a deterrent to crime. However, the traffic stop inter-mingles these two aspects of police activities into one very critical component. They keep us safe by reducing the number of hazards on our freeways, and surface streets i.e....speeders, and those citizens who may be inclined to road rage, or other dangerous activities while driving.

I don't really need to explain to you how seeing someone else pulled over by the police can shave a little bit of the lead off our own right foot. And if we witness it enough in any given area we call that area a "SPEED TRAP" and everyone slows down to avoid being NEXT, thereby the safety of the citizenry in that area is increased. That is how directed patrols are designed to work. But another aspect of the vehicle traffic stop is that it serves as a proactive way of encountering wanted, or dangerous criminals, and removing the threats that they impose prior to having to respond the call for help from the public.

> *"a different hybrid demeanor does show up at times in which the law enforcement officer who is sworn to uphold the laws of the land, and the constitution will become the miscreant offender who like a coward attack and at times even kill defenseless citizens."*

The vehicle traffic stop usually involves a Class C level infraction of traffic laws. A class C level of infraction is the lowest level of infraction in our judicial system. However, because it is also the most common, it encompasses a large cross section of our society. It is within this cross section that we will find custodians, doctors, soccer moms, factory workers, rapist, policemen, burglars, victims etc. Most of these people will give no resistance and usually their compliance will not be met with abusive behavior on the part of law enforcement.

At times a different hybrid demeanor does show up at times in which the law enforcement officer who is sworn to uphold the laws of the land, and the constitution will become the miscreant offender who like a coward attacks and at times even kills defenseless citizens. This is not always the case but it does occur. We will deal with this issue in an upcoming chapter, but for now the traffic stop must be broken down.

Most criminals will give little to no resistance during traffic stops just as an average citizen would not. *The most common resistance met by law enforcement is being lied to.* Many people do not consider that lying to a police officer as a form of resistance but it is. *Lying serves the purpose of preventing the officer from the successful performance of their duty.* This can be frustrating for the officer as it forces them to have to weed through erroneous information and take up more time than necessary during a traffic stop, or citizen contact. So it is safe to assume that lying to an officer can come with a price, in that it may lead to some retaliatory abuses on the part of the officer. *The officer is supposed to remain professional during the interaction but as will be demonstrated later not every officer is capable, or even willing to do so.*

During a traffic stop officers will witness citizens attempting to use verbal intimidation such as profanity, or insults, or accusations regarding the officer's integrity. Officers are frequently verbally antagonized as citizens attempt to manipulate the officer by introducing an element of confusion to the interaction. Occasionally this over load of elements is intended to disrupt the officer in hopes that he or she will miss something. This is done by experienced criminals who understand the process. The confusion that they induce by acting in a belligerent manner, or demonstrating a provocative nature will let them get by with some other infraction of the law by frustrating the officer. A few more will flee the officer, or even attempt to physically engage, or kill the officer.

There are also the manipulators who name drop, and get overly friendly, or engaging as they try and talk their way out of a citation. This manipulation can escalate from begging, and crying to offering sexual favors, or cash for leniency.

"... the police officer is a human being and comments about the officer's parents, wife, sexual preference, or small private areas will do way more harm than good."

Whatever the case may be the intentions of every person the police officer encounters must be discerned in a split second. ***In his book "Blink" Malcolm Gladwell brings to light some eye-opening research on the "art of thinking without thinking".*** Making decisions without a conscious step by step process based on concrete experiences. Experiences which have been proven correct enough times so that no debate is necessary for the outcome to be predictable.

No matter what ploy is used on a police officer he must correctly determine its true intent and only the weakest of officers will fall to these ploys. Each officer knows no matter what takes place during the traffic stop, no matter how sincere you may be ,or agitated you may appear to be at some point he will be the topic of conversation somewhere down the road with a group of your friends, and you will tell them all about how you buffaloed, or tricked him either out of a ticket, or into missing the bag of weed just above your visor or whatever it was that you did not want him to notice, or something you did not want him to do so that you could call him stupid later. You may even remember his name and tell them who it was.

I personally remember hearing a fellow on the street brag about telling a nervous rookie officer that his name was Levi Garrett. And right there everyone laughed at the gullible, and weak officer for writing a ticket to a can of snuff.

What is frequently not understood by the general public is that most police officers who have any experience at all have already seen pretty much anything you can think of including your act. Rarely will you be convincing enough, or original enough to get away with one. Unless of course you encounter the police officer who wrote the ticket to Levi Garrett. Whether you play the race card, curse, name drop, or whichever tactic you employ it is not amusing, and is most often considered an insult. These tactics only serve to increase suspicion, and invite further inquiry into your actions. Most seasoned criminals know this and they will tend to be the most cooperative. So the cooperative attitude is also an attempt to disarm the officer psychologically by getting them to relax and not be as sharp during the interaction. They may start with "hey don't I know you?" "You usually work the area my mom lives in." "Yeah she says you were real nice to her." It's a con job and a good police officer knows it.

The police are trained to already know when they exit their vehicle whether you will receive a citation, a written warning or given a verbal warning. This decision is not supposed to be based on whether they like you, or if they know anyone that you know or not. At times the citizen may feel helpless when it comes to the outcome of a traffic stop so the urge to damage the officer in whatever way they can becomes their only source of comfort as they are cited.

The police officer is a human being, and comments about his mother, wife, sexual preference, or small private areas may do way more harm than good.

The mental strength that it takes to walk up to a strange car at night, or up to a van with curtains over the windows on a long untraveled road is not one of invincibility, but one which fully embraces the true frailty of the mortal existence. And the police officer must still summon the courage to do the job anyway.

"You can hear your heart beat, you can feel your pulse, and you can hear everything. The dispatcher advised that the driver has a felony warrant for unlawful carrying of a weapon and they are waiting on a physical description to verify the warrant. Your back up is minutes away. You have already opened your vehicle door and released your shotgun from the rack. Police department policy says you wait for back up before making the second approach to the vehicle to verify that the driver is a physical match to the warrant. You just saw the brake lights come on. Will he shift into drive in an attempt to flee. You need to tell him to turn off the engine. He probably knows he has a felony warrant. Should you take your shotgun with you when you tell him to turn off the engine, and place the keys out the window? Back up is still not here. His reverse lights just came on he is going to run. You jump out of the patrol car, and move forward. You left the shotgun it would have slowed you down. You yell for him to stop, he slams on his brakes and opens his door. *You see the muzzle flash. You are falling now but it seems like you're falling in slow motion. You don't even feel yourself hit the ground.*"

Everyone cannot step into chaos and stay focused enough to survive. That is why every officer has to believe in his, or her training and experience, he has to be determined that he is going to make it out alive because he wants to see his children, and talk to his parents again. And the only warning he may get that harm is about to come his way is the wry smile a driver gives over his shoulder to a passenger in the back seat before the shotgun blast comes through the open window of the rear driver side passenger compartment. Game over.

Traffic stops are practiced over and over with different hazards being presented to officers in training from the guy with the shotgun wired to his door panel at just the right angle so that he can open his door and take your life as soon as your reach the area between his gas tank and rear door on the driver's side. Or maybe the rabbit who jumps from the vehicle and runs to distract you so that the driver can get away. Then there is the passenger who stayed in the car and just told you that the driver took the keys with him only to produce a spare key and get the same car with drugs in it out of the area before your back up arrives.

12.3 % of black drivers were searched while only3.9% of white drivers and 5.8 % of Hispanic drivers ARE SEARCHED...

The traffic stop is filled with a million variables and that's just for the good officers. I have a few categories I put policemen in. I will divulge these in a latter chapter. I would not dare to say that they are all inclusive but each category has their own differing paths and each officer has different ways of doing things when they come into contact with a citizen. For some officers, certain triggers have to occur to require him to search. While other officers do what they want with no regard for procedures. Sometimes it is race, sometimes cultural, and other times it can be a myriad of non- verbal cues, or other perceived data which will make an officer search a vehicle.

"Probable Cause" or" Standing" are defined as "Apparent facts discovered through logical inquiry that would lead a reasonably intelligent, and prudent person to believe that an accused person has committed a crime, thereby warranting his or her prosecution,"

I start this section in this manner because every legally executed stop ever carried out must began with this element being well established. There must be probable cause, or standing to initiate a traffic stop. This evidence, or violation of traffic laws can be a non-functioning brake light, a burned-out head lamp, an expired inspection sticker, or a vehicle being operated in excess of the speed limit. *When an officer chooses to engage a citizen he, or she must be able to communicate a legal, and legitimate reason for detaining you as per your rights under the 4th amendment of the constitution of the United States of America.* This element will become the basis of every search, confiscation, and arrest, and they are established on this primary legal requirement. This basic tenant remains although some recent court decisions have seemingly rolled back the once clearly established boundaries as per the application of this amendment. *Officers know the law and the ways around it so if a police officer wants to stop your vehicle they can find a myriad of ways to explain why they executed a vehicle traffic sto*p. And yes, sometimes police officers lie and no one can stop them but you the citizen. This will be explained later in the chapter on filing reports against police officers. Some of the lesser known charges are worn threads on tires, could not see the inspection sticker, license plate obstructed, cracked windshield glass, no bumper, damaged vehicle body from accident as related to the continued use of the vehicle on a public roadway, and failure to signal within 100 feet of a turn. The reasons are exhaustive but you get the idea.

If you are the passenger in a vehicle on occasion you may be asked for ID as well. I will cover this more thoroughly in a later section. I will caution that you do need to be aware of who you are riding with and who drives the vehicle that you are in. If there are a number of unpaid citations on a vehicle license plate number it will come up in the system. One lady I interviewed said that the officer came back and asked about the whereabouts of a family member with almost 10,000 dollars in warrants. She realized then that this family member must have gotten a ticket while driving her car and not told her about it. Had there been a male in the car with her he would have had to show ID. Even though he was not involved with the traffic violation he would have still needed to be ruled out as the suspect with all the tickets. This is an example of the information that officers know that the general population has no clue exists.

Many departments do not have a quota per se but they advise officers that an individual on patrol should see at least 2 violations per day. It becomes an unofficial quota.

It also opens the door for the officer to come off as a bully by demanding ID from everyone in the car and not telling them why as a way of flexing his official authority. If any resistance is given the officer may arrest an occupant for failure to identify to a police officer, again this is because he has legal standing in regard to information that he has which the citizen is not privy to, namely active investigations. If he is lying, and violating your rights as a citizen he believes that you are too dumb, or afraid to call him on it. Always, be polite but ask the officer why he needs your ID. If he gets angry, or abusive you know then he is a bully, a wolf, or a curse. Later I will give you information on the types of officers you could encounter, and provide more information as to the makeup of these policemen and their modes of operating.

In some states, you can be arrested for any violation of the law except generic speeding, unless you are an out of state driver and then of course it is up to the officer. This frequently depends on the officer's mood, whether the police officer is behind on activity for the month, and of course if the police officer believes that you are giving them a hard time when you question them, or assert your constitutional rights. Many departments do not have a quota per se but they advise officers that an individual on patrol should see at least 2 violations per day. It becomes an unofficial quota.

Daylight Traffic Stops

First let us consider the average daylight traffic stop. Depending on the circumstances of your interaction you may, or may not be personally observed by the Police Officer who pulls you over in a violation of the traffic laws of your particular state. I say this because in some instances the officer on the bridge with the radar gun is stationary and he calls another officer waiting ahead for you with a description of your vehicle and the violation he observed. Usually the officer who observed the violation has already signed the tickets so that he is the officer of record for the purposes of the court.

Beware unmarked police vehicles
attempting traffic stops in isolated areas.

In every instance, you should be made aware that a police officer wants you to pull over, be it lights only, or lights, and siren. Some officers will use only their lights and this is a generally recognized signal to the operator of the vehicle that a police officer is attempting to stop the vehicle they are operating. Even so I recommend being very careful of pulling over for unmarked police cars who turn on their lights to stop you. Some states have passed laws against using unmarked police vehicles for the purposes of traffic enforcement due to the dangers it exposes the public to at the hands of criminals pretending to be law enforcement officials.

Of late it has become the practice of drivers to call 911 when a policeman pulls them over. This is to verify that a unit from the jurisdiction that they are in is legitimate. It also puts the traffic stop on an official record that cannot be tampered with by the officer. If the officer has pulled you over without calling in the stop it becomes a record of his or her abuses, and rule breaking. If this is not a legitimate traffic stop officers in the area will be notified to get to you and investigate. If this information is divulged to the policeman or police impersonator who stops you it will certainly curtail whatever unlawful intentions they may have had.

In one recent case a suspect yet to be caught I might add, went online and bought a decommissioned police vehicle and installed his own lights and an insignia of the city he chose. The impersonator then pulled over, and tried to arrest a lone

Survive Police Contact

female driver on non-existent traffic warrants. The fake officer of the law fled when the female dialed 911 after he asked her to step out of her vehicle and get into the back seat of his squad car. Her quick thinking saved her life. Calling 911 to verify that an officer is a legitimate peace officer by asking the dispatcher is a wise practice when you have safety concerns.

While unmarked police vehicles are a problem for citizens, not every state places a priority on fixing the problem. A few states use almost no restrictions on the use of such vehicles, while a few more have attempted to reach a middle ground by requiring that some distinctive marking be displayed on all state government vehicles. In either case whether the vehicle traffic stop is initiated during the day or it occurs at night I recommend that the driver stop only if they believe that an actual police officer is pulling them over. *If there is doubt they should continue driving until they encounter a marked police vehicle, or get to a well lighted, or populated area.*

Once the operator of the offending vehicle becomes aware that they are being pulled over by a police officer it is mandatory that you stop immediately unless it is unsafe to do so. Further to that point use hand signals to let the officer know that you have seen them so that they do not have the misconception that you are running from them, or ignoring them. Failure to do so could result in felony evasion of a peace officer charges being filed against you. Now these charges may later be dropped if your counter argument is convincing enough to the district attorney or the grand jury. But you are still going to be out of a substantial amount of money. So be certain to signal the police officer that you have seen his lights. It would be a good idea to investigate the legal requirements in your state, and remember the statute numbers in case you are ever in this situation. I say this because when you quote the penal code to an officer you are signaling him that you know what you're doing and what he is supposed to be doing. This particular subject will be broached in a later chapter.

Look at the officer's weapon is it unclipped or in the ready position.
Read the officers name on his name plate and use it.

After your vehicle has been stopped the officer will position his vehicle in the manner in which he was trained. That is normally anywhere from 3 to 15 feet

15

behind the vehicle being stopped. The police vehicle may be as much as 2 to 3 feet further into the roadway than the vehicle being stopped. This allows for a safety barrier between the officer and passing motorist.

The officer may use his speaker system and order you from your vehicle and onto the rear passenger side of your car. Usually the ordering of a driver from their vehicle requires some other exigent circumstance. Frequently this irritates drivers especially when you don't know why you are being pulled over, or the weather is oppressively hot, cold or wet. Most police officers would prefer that you stay in vehicle as it is safer for all involved. In some departments, it is against department policy for an officer to order you from your vehicle unless certain criteria are met as previously stated. Some officers will abuse their power and do it for no legal reason. This leaves only reasons of race, culture, sex etc.

The officer may exit his vehicle and approach your vehicle from the driver side, or the passenger side. How the officer makes his approach to your vehicle is entirely up to him. There is no set way as long as he does so in a safe manner. Expect to be asked for your driver's license, and insurance, and in some cases your vehicles registration papers.

The officer will usually let you know that you were observed in a particular violation. It will be up to that officer if they will cite you for the violation, unless they are on a directed patrol and have been ordered to cite all violators. Officers are trained to already know what they will, or will not do in regard to citing you before they exit their patrol cars. This decision is supposed to made independent of your attitude, however I have seen some officers change their minds because of insulting, and disrespectful remarks. This is considered unprofessional behavior because the citizen's attitude or lack thereof are not supposed to be mitigating factors in the professionalism the officer is to demonstrate.

The officer may ask for an explanation of your actions, do you have an emergency, where you are going, is the information on your driver's license is current.

If you have moved you only have a set amount of time to get your driver's license information updated to reflect your current address or it is a citable offence.

There are many schools of thought on what you should do regarding questioning by police officers. Some believe that you should cooperate if you have nothing to hide, while others believe that any information you reveal is simply being too cooperative, and can lead to the officer abusing your rights as a citizen.

There are over 17,700,000 traffic stops a year in this country. That's just about 50,000 traffic stops a day in America.

Statistically the number of traffic stops that end in the citizen being abused or killed are very low. However, I once heard a man say that "there are lies, damned lies, and statistics." There are no statistical numbers for how many citizens are abused, verbally harassed, threatened, bullied, given tickets when they have not broken any traffic law, or who have elevated speeds added to the radar reading to raise the fine for the citizen. There are also no statistics on victims who have been set up or have evidence planted against them for the purpose of padding arrest records, or the number of falsely sworn affidavits that lead to illegal search warrants, or the jail house confessions sworn to by inmates who have been fed information by detectives looking to clear cases at any cost. The list of infractions of law on the part of law enforcement grows every hour of everyday and there are no statistics to tell that truth.

All the while there is a growing move to teach citizens not to ever offer any information when contacted by police. I say do not offer any extra information. If you find yourself in disagreement with the officer do not force the issue, set the citation for court, and fight him where he can't say you went after his gun, or that he smelled liquor, or some other illicit substance on, or about your person, or car in order to execute a search for the establishment of a deeper investigation. Be courteous, and cooperative but not overly revealing.

Some critics of police practices advise exiting your vehicle and locking the doors while you stand outside and conduct business with the officer who pulled you over. This tactic may look suspicious but it eliminates any allegations that a suspicious smell was emanating from your vehicle as well as the need to search for weapons which are now out of reach. It can however by its suspicious nature become a rung in the ladder of probable cause, or standing which leads the officer to ask for permission to search your vehicle. Also, if an officer believes your presence outside the vehicle is a safety hazard he or she may order you back inside.

Other pundits who stand on the 5th amendment right for a citizen to remain silent and not be compelled to answer also further advise that a citizen should give ID, and whatever other registration, and insurance information your state may require, and then refuse to answer any questions other than to verify that the information on the license is correct. This is done to eliminate the age-old accusation of detecting the presence of alcohol or some other illicit substance emanating from your person. If you use these techniques you can expect the average police officer to become angry, and sometimes very disrespectful. *The police officer's perception is that you are challenging his authority, and manhood instead of seeing you as a citizen exercising his, or her constitutional rights.*

Some police officers use the plain view method if you refuse to give consent for a search. Officers press their faces against the windows and peer into the vehicle sometimes even shining their flashlights inside in an effort to find anything in plain view. If a police officer finds evidence of a crime from looking into areas that are clearly seen without reaching inside the vehicle or moving anything physically it becomes grounds for a more invasive search, and investigation. So, the butt of a joint, or the handle of a gun visible from outside the vehicle are sufficient probable cause, or standing to legally search your vehicle without your consent, or permission.

For some officers, there are no constitutional rights on their traffic stops. If they want to search your vehicle they will do it even if it means making up some charge against you in order to do an inventory of your vehicles contents…in other words SEARCH

In most cases your information will be run through any number of data bases in order to verify that you are not wanted. Sometimes if it is a traffic officer on motorcycle he or she may not run a warrant check. If all warrants searches are clear a citation may still be written at the officer's discretion. Signing the citation is not an admission of guilt it only serves to acknowledge that you received the citation, and are agreeing to pay it, or take other steps to remedy the citation within the number of days allotted on the citation. The police officer may advise you to read the citation, or he or she may verbally give instructions as to the amount of time you have to respond.

> *"it does not matter what happened, or what you say happened,*
> *the only thing that matters is what I say, and I say you ran it."*

After the citation or warning is given the officer should wait until you drive away first. He may make notes on his copy of the citation in case he has to go to court regarding the citation.

Some police departments have been known to have a standing agreement with the court to make certain marks on a citation to signal the judge that you need a heavy fine. Sadly, this practice works against citizens as the court is biased in favor of the officer without even knowing the circumstances surrounding your citation. This kind of wink, wink understanding is another example of how the system is stacked against citizens even if the officer makes up the charge.

I vividly remember a story told me by a deacon at my church of how the police officer pulled him over for running a stop sign that he said he clearly stopped for. The deacon even said he made eye contact with the officer while at a complete stop. The police officer was directly across from him and was apparently on directed patrol to ticket anyone running the newly erected stop sign. When the officer told him he ran the stop sign my friend protested that it was not possible, and that the officer knew it was not so. The officer responded that "it does not matter what happened, or what you say happened the only thing that matters is what I say, and I say you ran it." Situations like this do more damage to the public's perception, and respect for law enforcement that any other interaction excluding the incidents of police officers being caught on camera breaking the law, or abusing and killing a citizen. And again there are no statistics on these incidents but there are millions of personal stories of officers blatantly lying on citizens. It has been unofficially established that the incidents of police officers abusing the public when it comes to ticketing is far more pervasive than anyone would like to admit. When one citizen experiences this kind of treatment that experience will be retold time, and time again for years. It will also taint the way in which those citizens, and others relate to, and view officers who had nothing to do with the previously described incident. These moments are repeated thousands of times a day across this nation.

Please resist the temptation to burn out and sling gravel back at the officer and his car. This will result in another ticket for "exhibition of acceleration". Never insult, or offer any type of bribe to an officer even if they open the door. It has been proven to the citizen's detriment on far too many occasions. ***The street is not the place to prove anything to a police officer.*** Telling an officer off so to speak will only give momentary satisfaction, and letting a police officer know exactly what you think of them will yield only a fleeting emotional release as compared to the exhaustive and weighty ramifications of the officer's arsenal of retaliatory options with which to teach you a lesson on the street. In short be courteous even if the police officer is not. Or as my old sergeant told me "don't piss against the wind"

In the photo below the trooper orders the man from his vehicle and demands ID, when the man turns to get it the trooper shoots him. Later saying that he thought he was going for a weapon. If you have to reach somewhere tell the officer where you are reaching.

Freethoughtproject.com

This same trooper was in a recent shoot out and was probably experiencing what is known psychologically as "memory echo" thus, his immediate response was to shoot before being shot

Memory echo is the vivid reliving of an event that mirrors one in which the actor or in this case the police officer has been previously. It is akin to seeing large snake in a field and then seeing a branch or stick in the same field a little later and then reacting to the branch or stick as if it was the same snake.

This incident and many others like it are due to the poor training given street officers, and the limited resources allotted to monitoring, and proper diagnosis of officers after traumatic events. Unfortunately, blatant disregard for human life is also a reason certain officers shoot unarmed citizens. Officers are not robots and they carry with them the events of every shift to the next event, and the next day, week, and year of their lives just as we all do.

The officers reasoning when questioned about this over reaction related directly back to the shooting incident in which he was involved a few months earlier. In every deadly force situations, there are indelible marks left on the survivors.

> *One instructor in the police academy told his class that he had*
> *shot, and killed a man many years earlier in the line of duty,*
> *but still from time to time all those years later he would still*
> *awake at night and see the man sitting at the foot of his bed.*

In the mind of the police officer pictured on page 20, he may have feared that he was about to lose his own life, or some other citizen was in grave danger of serious bodily injury, or death, thus his reasoning to protect his life, or someone else's with the use of deadly force in a situation that clearly was life not threatening.

> *Is it the driver's responsibility to engage the police officer*
> *in a safety conscious manner?*

The driver's actions were normal, and compliant but not very safety conscious. The driver possibly could have mitigated the officer's fear, and memory echo by telling the officer where his ID was. This action could have led to a much different outcome for the driver other than being shot several times by the police officer.

Is it the driver's responsibility to actively engage the officer in a safety conscious manner? It may not be, but it also may be the only way to simple get a ticket for a broken tail light in lieu of being shot. No one can guarantee that an officer will perform his duty in a professional manner but the price for a careless, or frightened officer can be devastating.

What can we take from this real-world experience?

Do not I repeat do not go reaching willy nilly around the inside of your vehicle especially at night. I say this for several reasons. From behind your car the furtive gestures that you are making can signal an officer that you are hiding something illegal, or reaching for something deadly. Your actions have given him just cause to ratchet up his perceived threat level during his encounter with you. Now he can remove you, and all occupants from the vehicle, and pat you down, and all your passengers, possibly cuff, and separate you and your friends from each other as though you were the worst of criminals. And this can be done without the officer ever telling you why. This is usually the tipping point for citizens who are arrested for disorderly conduct.

***He is the law not you. You may not understand the
triggers you hit from just reaching around the vehicle.***

The average citizen is going to demand an explanation for the officer actions, and they may even refuse to cooperate with the officer's commands. One of the passengers in the vehicle may refuse to cooperate with the officer because they don't feel they have done anything to be treated this way. ***Once the officer is met with resistance of this sort he will not back down. He will call for back up and he will ratchet up his intensity. No one is going to bully or cow him. "He is the law". The police officer is not going to explain his actions to you it, demeans him as an authority figure to explain to you the what, and why of the way he conducts his business. This is the element of ego, and hubris that he is trained, and indoctrinated in as a police officer.*** This belief system can often completely eliminate his humanity, and compassion toward you because in short you are beneath him. His ability to carry a gun and take you to jail makes you nothing to him.

***A furtive gesture is considered a suspicious movement
one with unknown, or masked intentions.***

22

A simple exercise to demonstrate what the officer sees from his perspective is for you to have a friend, or family member park their vehicle and then you pull in behind them. Have them reach for the glove box, or a center console, or under the seat while you sit in your car. What can you see? Nothing, nothing at all. If this is not convenient the next time you are at a traffic light watch the vehicle in front of you could you see the driver's hands if they reached for anything in the car. Now imagine this scenario as an after dark traffic stop. Imagine this same lack of clear vision in a low light traffic stop. This is what the officer sees when you start reaching for information before he even gets to your car. So, are you hiding a gun, reaching for a gun, or getting insurance documents? Now you know why he wants you out of the car with your hands on the hood while he searches the areas you reached into, and some you did not. Your movements give him legal standing to search without your consent. Do not reach until asked for information.

Another school of thought on traffic stops that has recently gained traction is to exit your vehicle with your insurance and id in your hand and lock the doors. This is one option to eliminate the possibility of officers saying that they smelled an illegal substance coming from your vehicle. Your being outside the vehicle may be interpreted as you trying to hide something. And the officer may try and use it for probable cause to press for a chance to search, or inventory your vehicle. An inventory is taken if the officer finds grounds to arrest you, and at that point he is responsible for the contents of your vehicle and your safety. You have the right to say no to any search of your property but if the officer has standing, or probable cause, or a warrant your vehicle can be searched without consent.

The Supreme Court ruled in April of 2015 that an officer can no longer hold a citizen that was stopped for a traffic violation and wait for a canine officer to come and do a walk around of your vehicle. The case was recorded as Rodriguez vs. United States. The case came before the court and was decided after Rodriguez was pulled over for erratic driving. The officer wrote the warnings to Rodriguez and then asked if he could search the vehicle. Rodriguez said no. The officer then called for backup canine unit and waited for them to arrive. The officer then took the canine from his vehicle and did a walk around Rodriguez car. The canine officer alerted on the vehicle, and subsequently methamphetamines were found and Rodriguez was placed under arrest.

The delay in time of Rodriguez having received the citation warning and the search was about 8 minutes. *Justice Ginsberg speaking for the court said "Police may not prolong detention of a car and driver beyond the time reasonably required to address the traffic violation." Justice Ginsburg also noted that police officers who stop a car for speeding, or another traffic violation are justified in checking the motorist and his driver's license. But a traffic stop does not give officers the authority to conduct an "unrelated" investigation involving drugs.*

The decision applies the 4th Amendment's ban on "unreasonable searches and seizures" and covers all the police--local, state and federal. This now opens the door to officers making citizens come into the station and take care of violations immediately. The state of Texas allows for an officer to require an immediate bond on any citation except speeding. By immediate bond that means to take you in and make you pay the fine on the spot. This rarely happens but some power tripping officers will do it if they can. Check your states requirements regarding immediate bond on traffic violations.

If the officer brings you in to have you immediately pay the bond then he is responsible for your car which means in Texas you may have your car searched, or inventoried to verify the contents thereof.

In another recent decision the *Arizona Supreme Court ruled that since medical marijuana is legal in the state that police officer can no longer us the odor of marijuana in a vehicle as the basis of a search for illegal substances*. This decision has not been before the United States Supreme Court but with the changes in drug laws some tried and true police tactics will fall by the wayside.

Speaking on the attitudes of police officers the sad truth is because these are not men who like to lose in any interaction with a citizen, and their egos, and pride can affect good judgment. They have been told that they are the law and if they have accepted this they do not view themselves as enforcers of the law. Remember by this point you are dealing with egos and pride. Intimidation will be used to teach you a lesson. I just smile at them and look them straight in the eye because if Christmas comes early it's all right with me.

In dealing with one zealous Trooper I literally had to remind him of the weapons retention policy he learned in the police academy as he attempted to step within an inch of my smiling face hoping to intimidate me because he was angry about me exceeding the speed limit by 15 miles an hour on a highway in the middle of nowhere. I used this tactic, in a calm voice with one eyebrow raised and a sweet smile the whole time. *"Officer in what part of the academy that you attended were you taught to disregard weapons retention safety and try and scare a man that will never fear you.* The officer's dash camera and mic were on. He realized that I was knowledgeable and he backed off. He also realized that I was not going into a body bag, or a pair of handcuffs that day. He wrote me a ticket, and got out of my face. I purposely did not blade him. Blading is when you take a fighting stance by turning your body to one side of an opponent in order to diminish any target or striking area available to him. I did not have to say or do anymore. Sometimes an officer will move to your left or right to see if you will establish or maintain a blade stance.

This little bit of baiting, can make you look like an aggressive individual. *Always face the officer full on, and avoid aggressive posturing even if you are expressing disagreement with the officer. Be aware of your tone when speaking it is easy to sound aggressive when we are in a disagreement,* so it is important to monitor your own tone. If the officer is speaking out of line call it to their attention but do not join them in disrespectful railing and insult. Behavior like this plays right into the hands of police officers who would do you harm.

You don't know what I know or what I'm doing!!! Yells an officer at a citizen as he demonstrates that the citizen's rights mean nothing.

If you do not consent to a search the officer may threaten to hold you there until a warrant is secured. However, I have not seen many occasions where a patrolman even knows how to write the proper request for a warrant, much less get one. It is just a ploy to manipulate you into complying with a voluntary consent to search your vehicle.

On certain highways across the United States that are known drug trafficking routes the state police will stop vehicles that fit a certain profile. Any minor infraction will do in order for a stop to be made in these situations. You will be asked for consent to search your vehicle, and luggage and a drug dog may be allowed to walk around your vehicle. You could be detained if the police officer feels that he has enough evidence to try and get a search warrant for your vehicle without your consent. Other than the situation just described it takes some pretty special circumstances to acquire a search warrant from a traffic stop. And they are almost always related to drug trafficking.

When people say that they don't talk to police officers on a traffic stop it can really stifle the verbal probing that occurs, and it appears to control the exchange in a way that most police officers are not comfortable with.

Survive Police Contact

Many citizens do not realize when driving down the freeway that the vehicle in front of them doing the exact speed limit while everyone else in traffic are speeding, may not be the goody two shoes that they appear to be but in fact may be doing so to avoid detection by law enforcement personnel. That is why on occasion you may hear people say I was not doing anything wrong, and they just pulled me over and asked to search my car. It is on the rare occasion that a citizen knows what the police know, or what the police officer is tasked with trying to get done on directed patrols. *This is where a little tact, and courtesy on the part of the police officer can go a long way in getting cooperation.* But that rarely happens because as I said before, and will say again they have been trained to believe that they are the law, in lieu of being enforcers of the law so you should expect no give and take during an encounter with them. People have been put through some very uncomfortable situations and when they are cleared they expect at least an apology for the inconvenience but it never comes.

In one recent case a citizen who had been arrested and searched filed a federal law suit because after he ran stop sign when leaving the parking lot at Walmart he was pulled over. *The officer accused the citizen of holding, or clinching his buttocks together after being told to step out of his vehicle for the minor traffic violation.* The officer used this as probable cause to accuse the citizen of having drugs in his anal cavity.

The citizen was taken to a local hospital for an anal exam. The doctor refused on ethical grounds. The police officer then took the citizen to another medical facility where *the citizen was subjected to an x-ray, 2 anal probes with the doctor's hands, three enemas, three forced, and monitored defecations, and a sedated colonoscopy involving his anus, his rectum, his colon, and his large intestine. None of the searches found any evidence of drugs. All because an officer believed that he was clinching his buttocks* on a traffic stop for the minor traffic violation of running a stop sign when leaving the Walmart parking lot.

There was no apology from the officer to the citizen. The citizen was awarded an apology of 1.6 million dollars in the settlement he received due to his unprecedented abuse at the hands of the police, and medical staff.

Treatment like this has become the impetus for some creative ways of avoiding contact with police officers all together. *Recently some people have posted videos of them putting their IDs, and registration, and insurance data outside their windows in plastic bags. This really infuriates some officers, due to the fact that they don't feel in control when you refuse to speak to them. Their police training, and personalities don't mesh well with John Q Public ignoring the standard operating procedures that are normally observed.*

When people will only say that they don't talk to police officers on a traffic stop it really stifles the verbal probing, and it appears that this tactic also takes away a certain amount of control that police officers are not comfortable with handing over to the citizen. The reactions of police officers who are subjected to these tactics can bring about serious ramifications for the citizen on the street. In fact there is a very good chance that the officer will find some sort of justification to demand that the citizen get out of their car for some sort of interrogation. If the citizen refuses it immediately opens the door for his arrest.

As I said earlier by exercising their 5th amendment rights they get around some of the overly used accusations like "I smelled a substance emanating from the vehicle which led me to believe that a violation was occurring." Or when the subject spoke I detected a slur in his, or her voice which alerted me that further investigation was needed to ascertain if the subject was driving under the influence. This tactic of only saying I don't answer questions or speak to the police eliminates the over used smell, and speech line from the equation. In one instance the driver in the video would only point to a paper with large print that said, "I don't talk to the police".

 I personally know of a man who carries his over-sized phone in his shirt pocket because the camera lens sticks out just over the top. He records everything. These are only three tactics of many which allow the citizen to take a little more control over the elements of the traffic stop that they a can safely influence for their own good and that of their families. Each of these techniques has its benefits and its draw backs, often depending on the type of law enforcement officer you are dealing with.

Overly aggressive officers do not like being shut down by American citizens exercising constitutional rights. In either case knowledge is power.

TRAFFIC STOPS AFTER DARK

Due to the nature and setting any traffic stop after dark presents an elevated risk to the citizen and the officer. The average citizen is completely oblivious to many of the dangers to both themselves, and the officers executing the stop. The evening hours bring with them elevated use of drugs both legal, and illicit. This is due to more people getting off work and consuming alcohol, smoking marijuana, or other recreational drugs as a relaxation method, or just to party with friends. One of the side effects of certain drugs is a drifting effect towards flashing, or blinking lights when driving. Oddly enough the red and blue lights on a police vehicle are like a magnet to people under the influence of this drug. I cannot count the number of times that I have read, or heard of police vehicles being run into from behind while doing a night time traffic stop.

action is faster than reaction

The darkness also presents very limited visibility for both parties. This limited visibility is one of the greatest liabilities when it comes to the after dark, or limited lighting traffic stops. *The ability to track a citizen's hands, and to recognize a weapon and then respond is greatly reduced within this low light environment. At times the light plays tricks on even the eyes the most experienced police officer. Police officers are taught that action is faster than reaction. The actions of an attacker who moves before the officer will usually be effective whether it is a punch, kick, knife, club, or gun attack.*

This is because the officer must first perceive the threat through signals sent from his eyes to his brain. His brain then must analyze the information and formulate the appropriate response. Finally, the officers brain has to message his muscles to move and then the muscles have to respond. Officers understand that the amount of time for this to process puts them at a severe disadvantage, and even more so in low light encounters. So frequently they will over compensate by being hyper aggressive in order to control a situation. It does not make their reaction time any faster but it allows them the facade of safety and control.

As with daytime traffic stops the citizen must be alerted that a law enforcement officer is attempting to stop their vehicle. This may be accomplished with the use of lights, or lights and siren. Just as with daytime traffic stops I would be very leery of any unmarked police car attempting to pull you over in an isolated area at night. If you find yourself being instructed to pull over in an isolated area. Make every effort to signal the officer to let them know that you see them by waving your hand, or turning on your hazard lights, and then proceed to a well-lighted area. *On occasion officers have attempted to file evading charges on drivers who do not pull over immediately. Having to follow you to a more appropriate location with better lighting can be considered bothersome for some officers. They may perceive that a citizen is trying to take control of their traffic stop. And this becomes an ego issue which puts you the citizen behind the eight ball.*

At night time, it is a good idea to turn on your interior lights, and roll down all windows as soon you come to a stop. This gives the officer a clear line of vision into the vehicle and lessons the chance of having an overreaction of force on the officer's part. Your safety conscious approach to the traffic stop may cause the officer to have increased suspicion. Some officers will believe that you have been handled in the past. That means you have an arrest record and are trying to throw them off by being overly helpful.

Some police officers will believe that you are hiding something like drugs. One former narcotics officer says that any car with a bible in it needs to be searched. He further stated that he had on occasion found drugs hidden in the bible on the dashboard or in the back window. I still advise young men who are Christians to carry their license in their small new testament bibles. If you fit the profile and do not smell like you just smoked all of Columbia it can help identify you as non-threatening. The officer will still follow safety protocol but hopefully his gun hand will be a little more relaxed. The reason for the shift in suspicion of religious articles in vehicles is because some people try and trick officers with religious paraphernalia. That being said in the right circumstance if partnered with other tips in this book it could save a life. In any case expect to have the police shine their flood lights, and flashlights into the vehicle. They are looking for any *plain view violations*. A plain view violation would be a joint in the ashtray, or an open container of alcohol in the console which can be seen by looking through the window, without asking the occupants to move anything, and without reaching into the vehicle.

Never start reaching for information before the officer asks for it.

These are the kind of things that give the officer "*standing*" or "*probable cause*" to search your vehicle, effect an arrest, or inventory of your vehicle. Once a driver is taken into custody the police officer is responsible for everything in the vehicle, just as the police officer is responsible for the safety and welfare of the citizen that is now in their custody. The *inventory* is to secure the property of the citizen until they can handle whatever legal business they need to. Some officers abuse their arrest powers so that they can search the vehicle of the citizen without their permission. The saying goes "You may beat the rap but you won't beat the ride." Meaning even if the police officer uses drummed up, or weak charges against you in order to effect an arrest what he is saying is that, "I'm always going to win on the streets". Although the *inventory is not an official search, if anything is found during this process that is deemed illegal it can lead to the police officer charging you with additional crimes.* Some arrest reports may not list any other charge as the officer may choose to pursue only the greater violation thus pushing aside his trumped up or false allegation that provided probable cause for the arrest in the first place.

All that the officer has to do is establish a reason to take you into custody. Remember I gave you a probable cause definition earlier. One of the older probable cause definitions is. *"That evidence which would lead a reasonable and prudent man to believe that a crime is being committed, is about to be committed, or has been committed is probable cause, or standing.*

Keep in mind that the gesture of turning on your dome lights and lowering your windows demonstrates a willingness to cooperate, and that you are safety conscious even if the officer does not perceive it with the way you intended. On the other side of the same coin, not being able to see clearly into your vehicle will always set off danger alarms in the officer's head. Just like in boxing it's the blow that you do not see coming that knocks you out. So, just as a boxer is trained to watch his opponent's hands, and chest, and to look for certain actions. In the same manner, a police officer is trained to watch the hands, eyes, and body language of anyone he encounters, and to watch for certain cues which may tip him off as to a suspect's unspoken intentions.

The more you reach around your vehicle the more suspicion you arouse. Don't move.

If the interior of the vehicle is too dark the officer is at a serious disadvantage, and if the officer encounters several people in the vehicle during the traffic stop he has a much more difficult task at hand. This is where the perceived threat to an officer can cost citizen's their lives. *If your license is under your seat, or in the center console of your vehicle tell the officer where you need to reach in order to get it.* Even if a police officer asks for the document you should tell him where it is before reaching for it. Remember it pays to be safety conscious at all times.

In low light, or after dark encounters some people get perturbed at the officer's patrol car flood lights being shined into their vehicles. These lights are blinding to the citizen. They are designed this way for several reasons. If you can't see and you happen to have nefarious intentions then you are at a disadvantage to carry them out. The officer is given the upper hand because he can approach your vehicle in relative obscurity, and this keeps you off balance. That is why some officers approach from the passenger side initially and then return on the driver's side. It is to keep the person they are ticketing off balance. Citizens are frequently frustrated at the seeming over kill of having police officer's bright flashlight beamed into their vehicle blinding them as the officer looks through their car windows. The brightness of the newer flash lights available to officers literally turns them into weapons of disorientation. They momentarily blind anyone who looks into them. They can become very intrusive as the police officer tries to examine the pupils of the driver eyes, and ascertain if there are any plain view violations. With this type of treatment, it is no wonder that the citizen becomes agitated, and is more likely than not to complain, or gripe at the officer. Statements like "Oh couldn't find any real criminals tonight so you decide to harass the honest citizens huh" or why don't you go find a rapist, or a burglar instead of screwing with me" seem appropriate for the situation.

These statements and others like them are protected under the right to free speech but they can lead to the citizen being run through the ringer so to speak by an unprofessional officer. *I vividly remember a citizen lighting into an officer's mother in some very disrespectful ways. The officer wrote him six citations for his trouble and his vivid imagination.* This same behavior is interpreted by some police officers as being threatening, and challenging and could easily lead to the police officer making a determination in his mind that you need to be arrested.

In many online videos citizens are shown to be mouthy, and defiant just prior to a police attack that takes things much farther than the citizens ever wanted them to go, as the officer becomes physically aggressive and bent on effecting an arrest. However, you choose to handle being pulled over at night always think safety first. Your primary job is to get home safely. With that in mind you must approach every encounter with law enforcement with a clear understanding of what is occurring. You *should know your options, and rights. Ignorance is not bliss, ignorance is loss and pain. Think safety first.*

CITIZEN ATTITUDE

The last traffic citation I received was for going 81 miles an hour in a 60 mile an hour zone. I was getting on the freeway and was still on the entrance ramp when I observed an 18 wheeler in the right hand lane. I decided to speed up and get in front of him this was all observed from the access road prior to the ramp. In the lane ahead of the 18 wheeler was a State Trooper. So the big truck was not speeding. I saw the trooper and adjusted my speed down and got behind him. The trooper was at least 30 feet below me when I first saw him so I felt I had slowed enough to avoid a citation. Not so.

The trooper pulled me over and approached my vehicle from the passenger side and announced that I was clocked at 81 miles an hour, and that this offense required a citation. I looked him in his eye and said "I understand." The trooper seemed momentarily stunned and he asked, "What did you say?" I again looked at him and replied, "I understand". He hesitated a moment and then walked away. His being taken aback by my "I understand" statement. This told me what I suspected he was looking for an argument of fact on my part so that he could pull the belligerent card but my calm demeanor and totally unexpected response threw him off his agenda.

My youngest son was with me and as soon as the trooper went back to his car he blurted out "that man lied you were doing 71 not 81." I told him "I know" and that is why I said that I understand. I meant that I understood that the trooper in this instance is a liar, and a coward who hides behind his badge to act out against the public because he can get away with it. I further explained that I did not want to put him in danger by confronting the trooper on his lie. My calm demeanor and peaceful frame of mind kept any possible arguments at bay.

Attitude can be the only barrier between disaster, and the mundane. Even if the ticket is fallacious a wise move would be to go for the uneventful. *Once an argument starts with a police officer you began losing control over the outcome. To challenge the average police officer could cause a sever attack of EGO.* The trooper returned, and I signed the citation and went on my way without any further incident. I could have asked how many feet up his radar was active above ground level seeing as I was at least 25 to 30 feet above his patrol car. I could have asked to look at the radar which should have still been displaying my actual speed.

In an interview with another driver who happened to be a school teacher. I was told that when she questioned the officer's information she was told by the officer "if you don't want to take my word for it you can walk back to my car. I will let you look at my computer you and then I will handcuff you and take you to jail."

As my son, and I drove away from the traffic stop *I asked my son whom the judge would believe when I set the citation for court. We both agreed the judge would believe the lying State Trooper* because of his position in law enforcement. This is too frequently the case, as judges and District Attorneys don't care to question the integrity of a peace officer, no matter how many times the news shows video of them breaking the law, and violating the constitutional rights of citizens and then lying about it. I went back and took pictures of the incline and the area where I was ticketed. I even attempted to mimic the 81 miles an hour that I had been accused of doing. I imagined that doing that in the dark and without any doubt the state trooper was clearly out of line. I told my son I was glad that he saw how I handled the interaction with the trooper so that he could witness how to neutralize attempts to bait an emotional response. *Never give them what they want remain calm, and in control. When citizens act out it gives off signals that you want a confrontation*. Some officers want this and are more than happy to teach citizens a lesson about pissing off the police. As a citizen you don't know how your acting out with an attitude will end for you. *Don't assume that the officer will remain professional if you open the door for abuses to occur, you don't know who you are dealing with*.

The photo below is of a police officer who had three
violent incidents in which citizens were assaulted, when his lapel camera was
turned off. The final incident, was the shooting death of a 19 year female who the
officer said evaded him, and pulled a gun. *Autopsy reports indicate that the fatal
shots had a trajectory which indicated that the young woman was laying on the
ground and the officer standing over her when he fired his weapon.*

Freethoughtproject.com

If the officers ascertains are true and the deceased female had known who she was
dealing with she probably would have handled the interaction differently. On the
other hand if the police officer was standing over the young lady's body before he
fired his weapon it would tend to look as if some physical confrontation had
already occurred which placed him in a dominant position and her on the ground.

Remember my story of the female police officer who was threatening me, and
saying that she hoped I had warrants so that she could take me to jail. Likewise
had this same officer decided to arrest me and take me to jail and to file a report
that I threatened, or tried to hit her it would not have mattered what I had to say or
whether I was innocent or not I would have a criminal record today for assault
against a peace officer, or resisting arrest, or worse even if I won the confrontation.

I did not want to fight her but the she was about to leave me no choice. I had promised my mom that I was never going to jail and that promise meant a lot to me.

This incident with the female police officer happened prior to the advent of lapel cameras, or dash cameras for police vehicles. As I drove away with my girlfriend, and my brother in the car we continued talking as though it was a normal outing. Over the years that have gone by only I knew how close I was to going to jail, or severely hurting a police officer, and becoming a wanted felon. *The officer almost ruined my life*, and hers. There was no doubt in my mind that I could incapacitate her before she could ever get to the weapons at her disposal. She was standing too close and her gun side was totally exposed. If it came to a wrestling match I had played football, boxed, and wrestled in high school not counting the street fights that were mandatory in my neighborhood. I did not want to fight her, but the she was about to leave me no choice. I had promised my mom that I was never going to jail, and now this police officer was threatening to put me in a situation that I could never comprehend myself being involved in. I won because no matter what I felt I knew that I had to keep the right attitude.

The right attitude is the one that keeps you alive, not the one that gets you into a fight with a man carrying a gun.

During the contact, I thought about the repercussions of close family members who made bad choices with law enforcement officers, and the toll it took not only on their families, and the years off their own lives. Some had even paid with their lives. My heart was racing, and I was trying to decide how to handle this abusive behavior. I had never been threatened by a police officer, or verbally abused the way she was doing. *Even if she did not mean a word of what she was saying, she was still forcing me to make a decision about life, and death with her abusive, and threatening words.* I was not going to let her take me to jail for no reason, and I knew that I could never allow her to kill me. I was taught to never threaten another person, and to take everyone you encounter at their word if they threaten you.

As with the State Trooper I decided to remain calm, I kept the right attitude. *The right attitude is the one that keeps you alive, not the one that gets you into a fight with an armed man.* I never raised my voice. I responded respectfully, and did not escalate the situation with this aggressive police officer. One of the tactics I used in this situation is actually taught in police academies I lowered my voice below normal conversational levels to make her have to listen to what I was saying.

Even when she talked over me several times I never raised my voice. *I have yet to see a police officer lower his or her voice as a control technique when confronted by an irate citizen.* They usually lean toward serving up a larger dose of whatever the citizen is serving, and they back it up with the powers of arrest and bodily harm. The female police officer eventually wrote me a citation and let me go. About 6 months later I heard that she had got seriously injured by another man that she had tried the same bullying methods on but who unlike me realized that there were other skills in my bag with which to diffuse the situation before resorting to physical combat.

This incident happened 33 years ago and I am sure that she has long ago forgotten my face, my name, and even the traffic stop itself. But I have remembered it for more than three decades, and it has affected the way I view, and deal with police contacts. It effects the way I taught my sons to deal with police contacts, and especially female officers. Little did she know, or consider that her frightened, and overly aggressive actions would have such generational, and far reaching effects.

I highly recommend using the officer's name when addressing them. If it is night time and you cannot see the officers name tag clearly just ask them. These safety tactics work even if they are obvious. Do not make the mistake of getting too close to the police officer as this may seem to be an aggressive move on your part. Getting the police officers name and using it when speaking with them serves the purpose of humanizing the contact, this coupled with a respectful attitude can go a long way to helping you survive. The police officer has been trained to stay detached, and function in an emotionless manner in order to avoid personal arguments. The officer is trained to say, "You were observed driving at 75 miles an hour in a 55 mile an hour zone." As opposed to saying, "I observed you" the emphasis is supposed to stay on what the driver did not and not the officer. This is supposed to help the officer maintain a professional demeanor. The drawback is that this way of conducting business also removes the human element from the identity of the citizen, and thereby increases the potential for unwarranted, and unlawful abuse on the part of the police officer.

Psychologically once a person has been dehumanized there is no guilt in the mind of anyone regarding their fate be it ill treatment, or some other consequence. So, again the survival technique that helps firemen hold it together in a horrific fire can be detrimental if an officer becomes too detached and begins to see citizens as outsiders or nonhuman subjects.

This flawed tactic that was meant to help the officer function efficiently usually falls to the dust after an officer gives in to anger, due to provocation by a citizen, and at that point everything becomes personal to the police officer, who as previously noted are not inclined to concede anything to the citizen. This is one of the reasons I feel that I cannot stress enough to use the police officers name if you can. The ability of the citizen to create some form of human connection can be a difference maker. This can have the effect of causing a subconscious shift in the officer's perception of you as a human being, and not just a subject, scroat, scumbag, loser, or jackwad. These are just a few of the names officers refer to citizens as when they tell their co-workers about pulling citizens over.

If you have ever seen the movie Silence Of The Lambs you will note a particular scene in which the parent of a missing young female actor is encouraged to use the girls name during a television interview, and to give details about the girls life in an attempt to humanize her to her kidnapper and make it more difficult for the person to kill, or harm the victim. This does actually work, and for the safety of your few moments with a police officer you should use every tool available.

I was taught how to use none verbal skills like these in school. I learned to sit on the front row, and position myself on the professor's right-hand side. Some estimates say that 90 percent of Americans are right handed so subconsciously the right-hand side is a favored side. Sitting in the front of the class says that I am interested in what they have to say, and laughing at the professor's jokes said that I believed that they were entertaining. All these actions had a cumulative and direct effect on the perception of my instructors, as it related to my attitude and invariably my grades.

Likewise, *your attitude with a police officer can make a world of difference in how a traffic stop goes.* When the officer is speaking nod your head slowly up and down it gives the indication that you are listening in agreement. It releases tension and avails you to a more positive subconscious view from the stand point of the officer. If you nod rapidly it give the impression that you are impatient with the speaker and want them to hurry. They will become subconsciously irritated with you. So watch you non-verbal cues when dealing with police officers. They tend to read nonverbal cues very well.

Not all police officers will react positively to your agreeable attitude, and your conforming mannerisms. But for the ones who do take to your cues it can make a world of difference. Some officers have had personal experiences in which the individual who was most cooperative was actually setting them up for a surprise assault. As I covered in the section on action being faster than reaction *the necessity to keep one's guard up at all times can become a hindrance to interacting with the public in a positive manner.* Do not take it personally if an officer is standoffish. There are a myriad of reasons to project an outward persona some officers are afraid, yes afraid of the citizen at times especially if they are outnumbered or not in an environment that they have full control over, or if the citizen possesses what could be an eminent threat to the officers safety whether it be due to the size of the citizen, or the attitude of the citizen.

Over 3 decades ago I particularly remember one officer who was small statured opening a conversation with a large irritated individual with a bad attitude by saying "I'm scared but I'm here. I am totally justified in shooting you right now due the size difference and no one would say a word about it, now turn around and put your hands behind your back." The irate citizen complied and the arrest was made without incident. This ploy could have backfired. The police officer opens up a conversation with an already out of control citizen by saying that he is about to shoot them. Some people are not afraid of being shot, so now what? *The attitude of the citizen can play a great part in the outcome of the contact with police.* As I said earlier you never know who you are dealing with.

I personally have had policemen apologize for having to write me a citation. The level of sensitivity, and concern for me as a human being was clear. His exact words were "I'm sorry but I have to write you a ticket, I'm on a direct patrol for people who are running this stop sign but I can tell you are decent young man. If you can't pay this you go down town and set this up for payments, they will accept what you can afford." The year was 1981. His integrity as a law enforcement officer required him to follow the directions of his superiors, but his ability to be humane left me feeling better about the citation than if he had been one of many officers who stalked my brother, and I through my neighborhood.

Often the perception of police officers, and the attitude demonstrated by one group of people is not a shared perception, by people in other areas. That is because of differing perspectives. In one neighborhood officers drive by and wave at the children, and others who are out and about as they patrol. While in other areas the officers wear sunglasses, and scowl at people that they pass as if they are trash.

Statistically this can be borne out as is demonstrated in the graph below which was taken from one major American city.

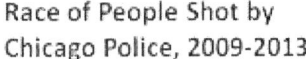

Race of People Shot by
Chicago Police, 2009-2013

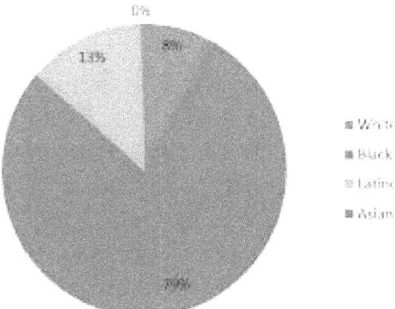

The chart above denotes the huge disparity in officer involved shooting incidents with minorities in one major city in this country. The question is how are the un-effected affected by this trend?

So the family in the Midwest who sees old sheriff Smith cruising by the family farm with fresh vegetables in the back seat of his patrol car have a very different perspective than the families who's nephew, or cousin comes home with a bruise on his head because he was harassed, and shoved into a wall face first in a stop and frisk that then turned into an illegal search for drugs, during which he had his back pack with school supplies dumped onto the ground and all its contents scattered out across the sidewalk. Adding fuel to the fire after being treated this way he is told to pick up this crap as the officer walks away laughing. The family knows that if the young man had made any aggressive physical movements the officer would have hurt him, or shot him and no one would have, or could have done anything about it.

It is easy to be on the side of law enforcement when all your interactions with them is waving and smiling. It is difficult to be on the side of law enforcement when you fear the police as much, or more than the gangs who hold your neighborhood hostage and operate with impunity on the streets of your community. At least the gangs claim to be looking for their enemies, whereas the police in your community will snatch up anyone they chose.

Usually it is the nature of people is not to get involved with issues that do not affect them. As the old saying goes when they came for this group I said nothing because I was not one of them. Then they came for that group and again I said nothing because I was not one of them. Then they came for me and there was no one there to help me. That appears to reflect the attitude of a large number of citizens, but not all. *Sadly there are not enough citizens who are unaffected who are willing to become involved in calling for a real and tangible change in the way the general public is dealt with by officers* as well as the way police departments across the nation identify and deal with officers who are a detriment and a liability.

Race hustlers need to be put on notice that the abuse of citizens goes beyond racial boundaries. There are clearly signs that one race more than any other tends to bear the brunt of the abuses but no one race has exclusivity on the scars that are left by the boots of the oppressive entity that has sworn to serve, and protect the citizens of this country. *So, the glaring question of social commentary is, are we countrymen or not?*

Another interesting note in the debate, and present climate before this country concerning its attitude, it's view of law enforcement, and the backlash of ill will which has not exclusively landed on the shoulders of those in the law enforcement community. One article recently noted that a seemingly good Samaritan stopped to help a young teenage girl stranded on the roadside with a flat tire. *When he saw a bumper sticker touting the "thin blue line" he turned around and left the young girl stranded. His remarks were call one of your dad's friends to come and give you a hand.* He drove away and left the befuddled girl in disbelief, and maybe a little afraid. *The attitude of the citizenry is transforming in ways that heretofore have not been seen in this country.*

Let's review the techniques I have covered so far.

1 Stay calm.

2 Speak in lower volume to answer questions.

3 Use the officer's name when addressing them.

4 Don't use aggressive language, body language this is known as blading or fighting stance, avoid excessive hand gestures.

5 If you decide to exercise your constitutional rights be respectful but firm.

6 If possible carry you driver's license in a new testament bible and make certain the officer sees you take your license from the bible. (the inference is apparent but if your car smells like cannabis, and you have gun under your seat this will not work for you, also if the officer has narcotics experience this may heighten his suspicion because some people use bibles to hide their stash in but it is worth a try. I used to carry my license in a pocket constitution. I no longer do so because the constitution means little to nothing to most Americans much less police officers who want to violate your rights.

7 Turn on vehicle interior lights, and let down windows if you're are being pulled over in a low light situation.

8 Don't attempt to be too conversational, or offer information that has not been asked for unless you really believe it will help the situation. Everything you say is being examined for inconsistencies.

9 Do not make up false charges on an officer, if something happens later you may not be taken seriously when you need to be.

10 Do not attempt to physically engage an officer unless you feel your life is in danger, and you have no other choice. A wrongful arrest can be remedied but a felony assault on a police officer is a much more difficult charge to deal with even if you were in the right.

11 Your compliance does not guarantee your safety, but your noncompliance can increase dramatically the chances of your being hurt, or killed.

12 Control your emotions. If you are riding with a hot head shut them down do not encourage them. One big mouth can get everyone in the car abused. You have options for addressing the officers violations, cursing him out is not the one you should use.

OFFICER ATTITUDE

It might seem wise to say that officer attitude is the barometer by which one may measure citizens attitude but realistically it is not true, and nor should it be.

An officer's attitude should always be professional. Officers quickly learn that professional language, and demeanor will keep them out of trouble for the most part. *Wise officers also understand that often a simple explanation to a citizen rather than an authoritarian/militaristic command style will garner much greater understanding and cooperation from citizens.* But officers just as quickly learn that not all citizens are not bound by the same code of ethics.

Sometimes police officers endure false accusations, profanity laden tirades, insults, and personal accusations not to mention physical threats against them, fellow officers and their families. Most officers adjust to the reality of the fact that citizen contacts are not always pleasant. Other officers drink the blue Kool Aid and began to believe that it is their duty to teach a lesson to any foolish individual who thinks that they have a right to say anything to the police that may come to their minds. Many citizens have learned the hard way that tit for tat with a police officer is not a wise game to play.

Officers do not take kindly to being insulted. The rookie, the overly aggressive female, the wolf, the curse, and the professional are all classifications I use for police officers. I do not think that they are all inclusive, and officers may move fluidly from one designation to the other depending on a number of mitigating factors. They all started somewhere, some of them were good officers once, some came into the police department with mental, and social deficiencies, as well as racial tendencies. These officers are tolerated in the ranks, and sadly in some cases even heralded as examples to be emulated.

Officers are subject to the same life changes and tumultuous twists and turns as anyone else. *An officer going through a messy divorce is supposed to be professional but is he more likely to be less tolerant and maybe even a little more likely to demonstrate an abusive tendency due to the private hell he endures.*

He will not be pulled back by his fellow officers
because in their world that officer is more important to them than you are. In their world it is them against the world and they cannot betray each other.

42

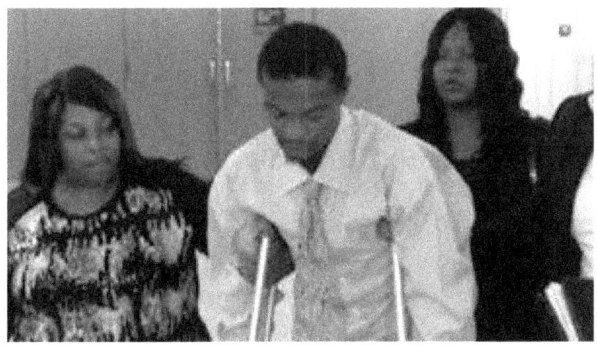

The lawyer for this man who was beaten, and attacked by a police canine says that none of the other officers present tried to save him from being attacked by their peer, or the dog that was used to maul him.

Officers who are not having success in their professional lives can be very agitated especially if the perceive they have been looked over in favor of someone they consider beneath them. (This is code for race, or gender bias.) On occasions the persons or gender of that perceived designation will be targeted consciously or subconsciously. This can be done under the color of law thus any actions taken do not appear suspect. In the movie Crash this is depicted over and over as a motive for the actions of multiple characters. So, the domestic dispute that could have been talked through ends up being handled with rough hands due to the professional issues an officer may be dealing with.

The minor traffic infraction becomes a citation rather than a warning. And a comment by a citizen that rubs the already antagonized officer the wrong way ends up getting the citizen taken out of the car and searched while they sit in the back of the police car in handcuffs for the officers' safety and that of the citizen. Not to mention the severe tongue lashing the citizen will endure from the officer as a way of asserting his dominance and authority on the street. And to demonstrate to the citizen that their fate rests in his hands so they should learn to keep their mouths shut because as I pointed out earlier *"you may beat the rap or small charge I bring against you but you will not beat the ride downtown or your car being towed"*.

Officer attitude is openly displayed in front of their peers. It shows up in jokes, and comments that should be checked by their fellow officers but will not be

.

The officer having money issues can pull over the Mercedes Benz for going 5 miles an hour over the speed limit and take out a small bit of revenge on a citizen who is more well off than him.

Likewise, the racist or sexist, anti-gay, or anti straight officer can exercise their biases without fear of reprimand, this is done under the color of enforcing the law.

I knew a rather attractive looking young woman who frequently complained of being pulled over on numerous occasions. She never got a citation and the officer always had a good attitude and she was let go even if she had a minor violation. My brother on the other hand never got a break. In fact, his experiences were the opposite, he was lied on, and ticketed so many times he felt he should have resorted to avoiding police as much as possible due to the aggressive attitudes of the officers who patrolled our neighborhood. Again, this was in the pre-gang era of our neighborhoods. Officers waited near our high school and followed young men from the parking lot to their homes waiting for the driver to make any kind of an error. Young men knew this and were very uncomfortable but at the same time ***they were powerless to stop the behavior because the police officer was doing his job.*** A senior officer confided to a relative of mine that some officer openly joke about how they show productivity for the day by getting behind African American males and following them until they make a traffic error.

With the silent approval of the upper level police department leadership no lower ranking African American police officer could make a stand without risking career suicide.
The abusive language and jokes about taking advantage of this powerless segment of American citizens went unchecked and became the norm, or the standard for rookie officer who were just finding their way as new police officers. The command staff was not oblivious to these practices, and sadly in their silence they gave their blessing for it to continue. With the silent approval of the upper level police department leadership no lower ranking African American police officer could make a stand without risking career suicide.

Officer attitude is openly displayed in front of their peers. It comes out in jokes, and comments that should be checked by their fellow officers, but sadly what I will call cowardice takes over. It is easier to give a little chuckle and walk away than to confront the racist, or sexist officer and take a chance of being labeled, and ostracized, or worse. When sworn police officers can openly brag and laughing about twisting the law and exercising no professional ethics and nothing is done then it time to clean house from the top to the bottom. And in my opinion the cowards should be swept out with the trash. *Not physically abusing an American citizen is no excuse when you hold the flashlight of the police officer who chokes out a non-combative citizen while he pleads for mercy right in front of you.* When officers use the driver changed lanes without a blinker, or they did not signal their turn within 100 feet, or the I could not see the inspection sticker as we passed. They are just excuses to pull over and harass a citizen and run warrant checks on everyone in the vehicle then they have ceased to be true law enforcement officials and have entered the realm of lawless bullies. My personal challenge to any sworn duty law enforcement officers is contained in the statement below.

> *Your silence makes you complicit in the abuses*
> *of innocent American citizens because you have*
> *chosen not to care about American citizens, or the constitution*
> *that you swore an oath to uphold!! Do the right thing*

Another important factor in officer attitude is **THREAT LEVEL AWARENESS.** This system was developed by Jeff Cooper and is still used in law enforcement to teach officers to recognize and identify differing levels of threat awareness. Threat Level is a term given to the perceived measure of an individual's immediate ability to present themselves as a physically imminent threat to the officer, or those around them. It involves taking note of their hands, body language, eyes, the area, and time of contact when the police officer encountered them.

When the officer encounters individuals, he must assess them quickly in order to determine their intents. Are they facing him head on? Are they turning one side to the officer like a boxer or a martial artist? This is known a blading. Are they shifting their weight from side to side? Where are their eyes focused? There are many other aspects to threat evaluation. Even the shape of an individual's eye brows can speak to personality type and the likely hood that they are what is known as fighters.

What tends to happen is that as a police officer moves from the first threat level known as **WHITE:** This is usually when you are with family and friends at home. It is a mindset which lends itself to being in a relaxed state of mind, without any situational or tactical awareness.

The second threat level is **YELLOW:** which is a relaxed but cautious watchfulness. Usually when officers are on duty this is their operating level. They watch the hands of people they encounter, they take note of anyone acting in a suspicious manner.

The third threat level is **ORANGE**: This level identifies a person, or situation of interest that the officer now focuses on. IE…Terry Stop, Stop and Frisk, Field Interview, or just watching a suspicious person loitering around the corner of a neighborhood store.

The fourth threat level is **RED.** Red is exhibited when the orange person you identified has gone further into a behavior which causes the officer to prepare to act against them for the safety of the public, or the officer himself. In short, the potential threat identified as orange has now become a potential target of action.

The fifth threat level of assessment is **BLACK:** It is a level I added in which the officer loses control and begins acting in a manner that is both out of control, and completely counter-productive to the office that they hold, as well as to the safety of the general public. This is most seen in the moments following a chase be it a foot chase, or vehicle chase. Many Police officers 'careers have come to an end at the end of a chase. But also in this category we have the officers who beat suspects, or who give the suspects repeated jolts with the taser when one would have done the job. Let me explain what I mean. Some tasers are set to deliver a jolt lasting a few seconds with each pull of the trigger, but if the officer pulls the trigger say five, or six times repeatedly the taser will multiply the 7 second jolt by the number of times the trigger was pulled. This tactic gives the targeted suspect a much longer jolt. Once the process has begun it is known as taking, or giving the "full ride".

One recent occurrence of an officer operating in a black threat level was demonstrated when officers tried stop a senior citizen walking down the sidewalk. The slightly built man was visiting from a foreign country and spoke very little English. When he was approached by officers he was able to say, "no English, Indian" He was also able to give his sons address and point to his son's house. The language barrier was problematic for the officers who did not attempt to contact anyone at the address the man had given and pointed to. As the confused man attempted to walk on the officer threatened to put him on the ground in English. Dash camera video shows that as the 57-year-old slightly built man turned away from officers, he was lifted off his feet, and body slammed to the concrete by a police officer causing partial paralysis due to spinal damage. Several officers were there on the scene as the video shows them trying to force the subject with a spinal cord injury to stand up after placing handcuffs on his limp body. The officer could have grabbed the man by the arm and pointed at the ground signaling him to stay there as he mouthed the "stay". I know this is Monday morning quarterbacking but it does not take much of a brain to recognize a wolf on a power trip when you see one. The photo below is a prime example of what a police officer operating in a black threat level awareness mind set is capable of no matter who he is dealing with. Merciless, ruthless, thoughtless.

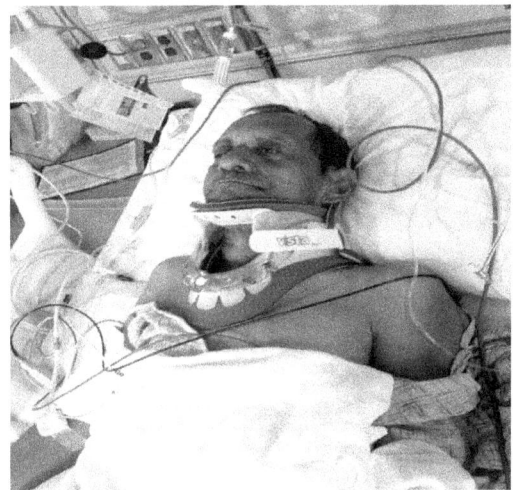

Freethoughtproject.com

When the officer acts out in a hyper aggressive manner with little to no justification for his actions, thus placing the lives, and well-being of the public he has sworn to protect in great danger.

they either see a threat which does not exist, or they make up the threat to justify the cruel, abusive and murderous actions that they have taken, or desire to take against the public at large.

Case two occurred at a Walmart store in an open carry state. A call was placed to 911 by an overzealous employee, who may have lied about the victim's actions. Upon arrival at the store police located the victim, he was talking on a cellphone with the pellet gun pointed down at the floor. The pellet gun was sold in the store as a toy. Other reports indicated that it had been on the shelf for 2 days prior to the victim deciding to purchase it in its unwrapped condition. The victim was not found pointing the pellet gun, or threatening any other customers as had been reported to the 911 operator. No other customers were near him. The officer's obligation was to make contact with the victim, secure the weapon, identify the victim, and verify that the allegations were correct before taking appropriate actions as codified by law. Video evidence shows that the officers shot the victim in less than 1 second after making contact with him.

freethoughtproject.com

Does this look like a police contact, a firing squad, or an execution?
The officer opens fire in less than 1 second.

The state attorney general released a public statement that the man was not in violation of any state laws because the state is an open carry state meaning it is not illegal to carry a long gun in public. *The attorney for the victim's family contends that less than one second was not enough time for the victim to recognize the police officers' presence, or comply with the police officers' commands.* From the i store video it appeared that the officers were behind the victim when the shooting occurred. These officers clearly departed from any reasonable protocol, and slipped into a deadly mindset demonstrating a threat assessment of black in which they either see a threat which does not exist, or they make up the threat to justify the cruel, abusive and murderous actions that they have taken, or desire to take against the public at large.

Below is a photo taken during a rarely seen example of an officer attempting to justify murderous intents can be seen and heard from a video referred to in the *freethoughtproject.com*. In the video it shows officers forcibly enter a citizen's car and began assaulting him. The citizen's hands were clearly in the air prior to the officer breaking into his car. The officer's weapons are drawn and trained on the victim. After entering the frightened citizens vehicle one officer can be heard yelling "stop trying to take my gun", "get off my fucking gun" as he pummels the frightened citizen with his fist. Every officer knows that if anyone grabs for your gun you secure the weapon with your dominate hand you do not keep throwing punches, and leave the weapon open for an attacker to wrest away from you and use against you, or your fellow officers. This cry is clearly fictitious and now opens the door for the citizen to be shot by either this officer, or one of his counterparts as a deadly force situation has developed. Once an officer feels that his life, or the life of anyone else is in danger he can legally take whatever measures he deems necessary to "stop the threat" i.e....take the life of his victim.

freethoughtproject.com

Incidents like these are unfortunately a daily occurrence. However with proper training they could easily be avoided. One major drawback is officers on the scene seem hesitant to pull back another officer who may be more aggressive than the situation calls for. Police officers must be given permission, and authority to stop a fellow officer who is out of control. Evidence suggests that in most cases of a citizen being abused, or killed unjustly there are in the vicinity other officers standing by, and allowing the abuse to occur without any interventional efforts.

As an officer accesses these higher dimensions of threat level assessments, and maintains them for extended periods it becomes harder to decompress, or wind down even in his personal life. When this overtakes him he will approach your car with your family in it having his hand on his gun as though your four year old is carrying an assault weapon. He will order you from the car, and give the command for you spread eagle on the ground in your best Sunday suit, and show no remorse for his actions regardless of your inconvenience.

One close friend of mine who is a pastor wished that he had been so lucky as to have just been ordered from the car, and placed on the ground in a spread eagle position. ***What he got instead was a gun placed in his ear as he was asked where did you steal this car? The car displayed a bumper sticker from a prominent college in the area.*** The pastor replied that his brother was a professor for the college, and that he purchased the car from him. The officer replied that "niggers don't go to" and named the college. It appeared that the pastor was a few moments from being shot when a backup unit pulled up, the police officer quickly put his gun away before the backup officer could determine what was occurring, and told the pastor to "leave now". Thankful to just be alive he drove away as quickly as he could. As he related the story to me I could feel his pain, frustration, and anger at being who he was, and being as helpless as he was against a police officer who was looking for someone to frighten, or kill for absolutely no reason.

As men our egos can really take a blow when we are diminished, or abased in such a provoking manner by another man. Especially when due to the station of our abuser we are made to feel helpless, as though we need to beg for that miscreant's permission to live. Just as the overly aggressive female officer had done with me the abusive male officer has made generational indentation on the way this man views and relates to police officers.

In hind sight as I reminisced on this story I surmised that the backup officer would not have gone along with the abuse, or murder of a citizen for a bumper sticker. The offending officer knew this, and was given no choice so he hurriedly put away his weapon, and barked "leave now". This was his attempt at covering up his murderous, or abusive intentions toward an innocent citizen who happened to be black with the wrong bumper sticker on his car. As you will note I mentioned earlier that police officers can, and will act out their prejudices under color of the law. This is easily accomplishable with little to no recourse for the citizen. It often goes un-noted as it boils down to the word of a sworn officer of the law against an ordinary citizen. And in most cases the courts will side with the officer due to his position of authority.

"I get paid not to trust anyone."

Survive Police Contact

When you encounter an overly aggressive police officer more than likely this officers attitude toward you is a reflection of his world view, his life circumstances, and his pain. The best advice I ever heard a police academy instructor give a classroom full of cadets was ***"beware when you look around and all your friends are cops."*** This usually means that you have adopted a ***" them vs. us"*** attitude and most of the citizens you encounter will be in the "them" category. In the "us" category you place people like yourself. People who are trying to get through another shift without getting hurt, killed, or sued, people who know your struggle. Most police personnel cannot go home and dump on their wives the things they see on any given day at work. The things they are helpless to fix, or control. Most police spouses would never enter a heavily wooded park after dark looking for an armed, and dangerous suspect, nor would they want to know what the inside of meth addicts house looks, and smells like, or hear the story of dirty feces encrusted diapers are piled high in a corner on top of the meth addicts stash. Nor would they want to hear of the baby holding a bent spoon, and putting it in their mouth totally oblivious to the fact that it was the spoon used to shoot up in earlier that day by their addict mom and her pedophile boyfriend.

When your life revolves around situations like these, and even darker ones that you have to live with on a daily basis, you will find it difficult to have friends who can relate to the pessimistic attitude of a man trapped in a yellow threat awareness level. That police officer has seen one too many crime scenes. Everyone becomes a suspect, and in his world trust does not exist. One officer said, "I get paid not to trust anyone." This is the reason police officer's divorce, and suicide statistics are so high.

There are many variables in determining the attitude of a police officer, just as with any citizen. But not one of these variables should affect professional demeanor. And with that being said I can guarantee you that the way you are treated will be affected by situations, and circumstances far beyond your ability to control or foresee. The following are in no way all conclusive but are examples of 5 personalities that I encountered in my teen years, as well as my time in law enforcement, and my time away from law enforcement.

THE ROOKIE

The rookie who has little to no real street experience, and for whom on the job learning makes up the largest part of his day. He is trying not to forget his training but invariably he will forget something anyway. I remember feeling my car shake as a young officer checked to make sure my trunk was closed so that no one would jump out and ambush him. I laughed because I remember hearing the same story and being cautious of everyone's trunk.

...the blue kool aid can and will make an officer believe that he is the law instead of an officer of the law. Take no guff cut no slack hook 'em, book 'em and don't look back

I just laughed to myself as he used everything he remembered from the academy as though he was on some high level drug bust. He does not know enough to be mean yet but to make up for his sense of inadequacy he can be overly controlling, and at the same time somewhat tentative in his demeanor. His attempts to prove that he is in control are not natural due to the tenseness in voice, and body language. If you interrupt him he starts all over on his practiced commands. If you really try you can frustrate him with questions that he is not practiced at answering. Ideally he is less dangerous however his biases can make him insensitive. If he has inferiority issues, or if he has consumed too much blue kool aid he may try and act with excessive bravado. In order for him to believe he can do this difficult job he has been psyched up by his trainers, and himself to think that he is the law instead of functioning like he is here to uphold the law. Statements like **"you may beat the rap but you won't beat the ride."** **"Take no guff cut no slack hook 'em book 'em and don't look back"** have caused him to have a misshapen self-image, and have tainted his mission to uphold the laws of the land, and the constitution itself.

It would appear that police jargon, and sayings like these, coupled with the mentality that goes along with them are the seeds that began the twisted thinking that get citizens hurt, abused, and or even killed despite situations which present no evidence of any laws having been broken because you are not supposed to "POP" Piss Off Police. This is how a rookie goes from being a young officer to a young wolf in uniform.

The following image is of a 76 year old auto mechanic who was being illegally arrested, slammed onto the hood of the patrol car, before being slammed to the concrete, and tased. The 76 year old man was pulled over when the officer observed an expired inspection sticker on the vehicle he was driving.

The officer was in the process of ticketing the driver. During the exchange, the driver showed the officer the dealer tags on the vehicle which he was legally test driving after repairing it. The state law in Texas exempts vehicles which are dealer owned, and under repair for the purposes of getting the vehicle ready for sell from being required to display a valid inspection sticker as long as the vehicle is being repaired, or tested and not being used for personal errands or transportation.

The officer is not a rookie but he has decided that he is the law. The senior citizen was slammed onto the hood of the police vehicle and then to the concrete after which he was tased twice. This becomes another example of you beating the rap, or the charge but not the ride to jail, or the towing, and storage fees on your car. The penalty for POP. (pissing off the police)

This kind of attitude is widely engrained into rookie officers and they carry it throughout their careers to the detriment of the citizens they have sworn to protect, and serve.

THE AGGRESSIVE FEMALE

The next officer profile that I have identified is the overly aggressive female. The motivations for this officer are usually fear, and insecurity. The perception of being physically weaker, or too sensitive can push many female officers to hyper compensate by assuming an ego driven aggressive stance that is purely defensive. It is done to win or maintain the respect of her peers who are mostly male. She needs them to believe that she can handle herself, and will wade right into a brawl with them shoulder to shoulder and hold her own. These are women who know that their male counter parts have suspicions about their physical fitness, and toughness when it comes to the realities of working the streets. I have information about one rookie officer who during the academy was asked by his instructor to physically embarrass two female cadets during the demonstration of a takedown. The female cadets seemed soft, and unprepared to survive on the street. And if she could not survive she becomes a liability to her safety, and the safety of her fellow officers.

I have personally witnessed overly aggressive female officers who felt they had to take control of the traffic stop by threaten, and trying to intimidate citizens. This is done to avoid being challenged or hurt. Once this attitude is taken by a fearful female officer she cannot back off, and step down her rhetoric no matter how cooperative the citizens are because then she will look weak. This is usually done when she encounters a male who physically dominates. The officer feels a need in her mind to establish herself in a position of superiority that should automatically be given by virtue of her position as a peace officer. However, on the streets this is not always the case and if she does not establish her dominance, and control of the interaction she opens the door to more opportunities for miscreants to act out against her.

Female on female traffic stops rarely illicit this cowardly survival technique. Female police officers who assume the mantle of being a tough street cop have not thought out the consequences of their actions or they simply refuse to consider any of the down the road consequences of their actions on other officers who come into contact with the same people that she has mistreated. In short, she just wants to survive, and the thought of her mistreatment of a citizen costing one of her fellow officers does not even factor into the equation.

Survive Police Contact

Female officers can make excellent officers, but due to the physical nature of the job there are certain situations which can overly expose areas of their make up as women which few women are capable of overcoming.

My encounter at 19 with one such officer started with her accusing, and failing to convince me, and herself that I was attempting to evade her new patrol car in my old hooptie. I ask her where did I turn? I had been on the same road for almost 2 miles and to evade her surely, I would have executed a number of available opportunities to turn, or pulled in somewhere but she found me at the next traffic light waiting on it. She was somehow able to gauge from my reaction, and explanation that no such thing occurred. Having dismantled her feeble attempt to charge me with evading she then actually began saying that she hoped that I had warrants so that she could take me to jail, all the while resting her hand on the butt of her gun.

Her attempt to establish control led her to come at me with even more paper-thin accusations which even she knew were unfounded. Each time I used calming techniques to redirect her, and thereby bring an end to the confrontation. She was barely 5 feet tall, and she had broken every rule of weapons retention, and safety taught in the Police academy. I knew that I could render her unconscious, and disarmed in a couple of seconds but that was not how I wanted my life to go. Later I will revisit this incident and explain more about the techniques I used to calm the situation, as well as how she came to some of her conclusions prior to her provocative attempts to bait me into her trap.

Far too many female police officers conduct their business in the fashion described above. The following picture could have been me at 19 but for the skills I taught myself in dealing with aggressive officers.

This citizen ran from a traffic stop. The female officer caught up to him and tased him twice as he lay face down on the ground. When the citizen did not respond to verbal commands he was shot twice in the back. The officer said she "feared for her life".

The female officer had several options available to her as he had the tactical advantage already. Once the officer's taser was deployed she would have had to call it in. This means backup and a supervisor should be expected. The fact that she is a female officer the chivalrous male officers could be counted on to make their way to her location post haste. Since the deployment of the taser had been successful if the prongs were still attached to the suspect the officer could have reengaged the shock component of the taser with a simple pull of the trigger. The officers tactical advantage in that with the suspect being face down on the ground was that she only had to position herself on the suspects blind side and wait for back up with her service weapon drawn and at the ready in case taser prongs had come out during the suspects fall. Numerous options existed that did not require firing into the suspects back as he lay prone on the ground.

Frequently the bravado demonstrated by the aggressive female officer comes from knowing that their male counterparts will soon be lurking in the area just to make sure that they are not having any problems. I have seen female police officers with 2 back up cars of officers within minutes without even calling for it. Some departments encourage the drive by check on traffic stops just to check on the safety of its officers regardless of gender. Add to this the nature of police officers to protect their own, especially the women officers, and it becomes a scenario that boils down to *when my back up arrives they are not coming to talk you down, they are coming to beat you down.*

Female officers can make excellent police officers, but due to the physical nature of the job certain situations can overly expose some of their physical weaknesses. *A smart female officer can do an excellent job, but one with something to prove, or who does not know how to take charge without being abusive can be bad news for the citizen, her fellow officers, her department, and the city she serves.* Even affecting families on a generational level.

The attributes that would make a female police officer effective in law enforcement are not the attributes that are praised. One incident I remember vividly was of a male driver having a low blood sugar event at a gas station. He was behind the wheel of his vehicle and unresponsive to verbal commands. He appeared to be inebriated for all practical purposes. My training officer said we would arrest him for DUI. A hardened street cop only saw another dirtbag alcoholic. About that time a female officer pulled up and she recognized the symptoms of a diabetic event and advised us to call an ambulance. Her attentiveness to the condition of the man possibly saved his life. She has been the rare individual of the female persuasion that I have encountered who could handle being a police officer. Her keen senses and quick actions are to be celebrated as she did not stand by and allow a citizen to be hurt due to the inability of a male officer to recognize the difference between being inebriated, and being on the verge of a diabetic coma. I never saw her again but I never forgot her good police work that day. *This same training officer once arrested a man with a broken neck for public intoxication and threw him in jail only to find out 4 days later that the man had fallen from a train and was in need of serious medical attention.* And this was the person trusted to train incoming rookie officers and guide their development when it came to dealing with the public.

THE CURSE

This is the officer no District Commander, or District Supervisor wants. This officer has survived by the skin of his teeth for so long no one even knows why he still has a job. He jokes about knowing where the bodies are buried as the reason that he seems untouchable. He may have been a good police officer at one time, but those days are well behind him now. He can see retirement getting closer and he does not care anymore. He will drive right by a store with a broken front window on midnight shift and hope that the owner does not find out and call it in until his shift is over so that the next guy can handle it.

The Curse has consumed too much blue kool aid, or he has seen far too many dark things to the extent that his perception of the world at large and even his own character has been diminished. This officer is a headache to his leaders, and to the citizens he is sworn to serve. He remembers when you could do it the old way, and your sergeant would tell the citizen that you would be fired, and then meet up with you and laugh off the whole complaint. I went on a call with a fellow like this to a domestic disturbance at a gay household.

After the call was completed he could not stop teasing me for being concerned about the safety of both partners. His jokes were endless, and I frankly could not wait to get away from him.

He naps on the job, and knows every hiding place in the city

He is typically racist, and sexist, and proud of it. This is the guy who swore that he knew Miss Americas phone number when Vanessa Williams became the first black Ms. America. It was fi, fi, fo, fo, fo, fi, fi. (A racist reference to Ebonic pronunciations)

When you are the law, you make the rules.

One such police officer was recently exposed when a black female who was in the middle of a domestic dispute. The woman flagged him down as she was trying to escape her abusive partner, and instead of protecting her he drove away and did not get involved after saying that he was on another call. The estranged boyfriend was later killed after pointing a gun at another police officer.

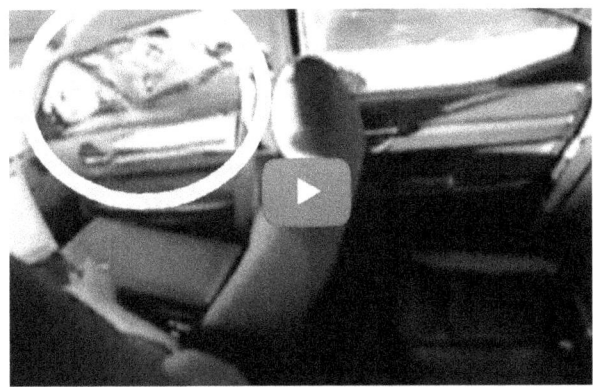

Freethoughtproject.com

The stories of these officers are endless but the effects of their negligence, and abuses cast a long shadow. I've seen police look at bleeding women, and then walk away and tell her husband to "handle his house". It is against the law, but when you are the law you make the rules. ***On a traffic stop this guy will take your weed and tell you he is cutting you a break.*** He half does most of his job duties and when he has to write a citation you better believe he is angry. He is most angry about having to show productivity on a directed patrol. That means everyone is getting a citation unless you are a good looking female. He does not apply current training to the accomplishment of his job duties. He does policing his way. He went through the academy with most of his superiors and he may have pulled their "asses" out of the fire a few times when they worked the street with him. So, they owe this slob with a badge in some testosterone driven manner, and maybe that is why he hangs on to his badge. He naps on the job and knows every hiding place in the city. He has low regard for minorities, and women and it shows. He makes rape jokes about the call his fellow officers are on. ***I overheard one such officer say, that the way "the woman looked she should have been thankful for the attention." He said it in ear shot of the woman who had been raped.*** He will shoot you, he will shoot you, he will shoot you. His personal life is usually a wreck and it puts him in a bad mood which he tends to take it out on anyone he has power over.

THE WOLF

The next officer is the one who has something to prove, he is a policeman for one reason, and that is to prove that he is the baddest mother shut your mouth on the planet. He is the one who will beat you for not signing a ticket. He sees every move you make as a furtive gesture (suspicious movement). And he will swear to in a statement and testify to it in open court without batting an eye. He will say that you put him in fear for his life, which justifies your being beat, and or tased if you are lucky, and shot if you are not. His favorite trick is to bait you into an argument with questions like *"are you all right, you seem agitated"*. Once you answer in a belligerent manner he uses it as the impetus to further investigate as to why you are so hostile, could you be under the influence of some drug, or are you of sound mind, maybe you are suicidal, or maybe you intend on harming someone else. So he instructs you to get out of the car. You refuse to get out of the car because you feel that he has no right to give you that command. Your refusal is met with physical force, and you are arrested, and charged with resisting arrest, and failure to follow a lawful command from a peace officer you are ticketed, and your car is towed at your expense. I have encountered this line of questioning on numerous occasions. That's why told the state trooper that I alluded to earlier "I understand" its ambiguous and open ended. It leaves no room for an interpretation of ill will. It was my response to his explanation as to why I was being pulled over and written a citation that was clearly a number he pulled out of thin air. He expected an emotional response and accusations of unfair treatment. He knew he was lying so my response was "I understand". As I explained to my son I understand that he is a liar, and a bully who hides behind a badge to act out his evil desires under color of enforcing the law. *Your answer must be strategic, and not emotional.* An emotional answer to the wolf may get you tased, clubbed, punched, or choked. Sandra Bland can attest to the powers of a police officer who is looking for chance to do harm to a citizen. Even if you make it before a judge your word against the word of a sworn peace officer will not carry enough weight to sway a judge who is already pre-dispositioned to go along with whatever the law enforcement official says. I am often led to wonder how this officer could pass the psych test to become a police officer.

You mean nothing to him if you are not a cop...

He not only drinks the blue Kool Aid. He makes a fresh pitcher every morning and drinks it butt naked in the mirror with only his gun belt on. He considers shooting an orgasmic event, and he is proud of it. His secret dream is to kill a suspect with his bare hands. He wants to be acknowledged for his fearless behavior, and thereby garner the respect of his peers. You mean nothing to him if you are not a cop. *He will volunteer to work the toughest neighborhoods because he craves action.* This officer becomes depressed if he does not get into a chase, physical altercation or draw his weapon on someone each shift he works. *"I will gun fuck you in New York minute, don't fuck with me."* This was a police officer's response to a young man who was back talking the officer.

He may have been a brave soldier in the war, but he has no place on the street. He may have a clean jacket in the police department files but he is far from a good officer. When his files are reviewed he looks exemplary but behind the scenes he is the worst of the wolves in uniform you will ever encounter. He is the dirty little secret in law enforcement that they don't want citizens to know about. And certain department heads in the police department want that kind of officer in their squads, and will protect him. This nightmare of a policeman is one of the reasons I am writing this book. If it helps people understand the game behind the game, and stay alive, and out of jail then I have accomplished my task.

Pictured below is mentally ill woman of about 130lbs who was shackled, handcuffed, and masked with a face shield to prevent spitting. While in custody she was then tased 4 times. Which stopped her heart, and respiration.

This is one of many victims of the wolf mentality. Her humanity stripped away she became nothing more than a thing to her jailers. I'm sure her screams, or groans meant little to nothing as she expired beneath the heels of their boots. The

manufacturer of the taser that was used recommended not using the taser more than three times is succession. It takes a special kind of mean to abuse the mentally ill.
SHAKLED, HANDCUFFED, MASKED, TASED AND DEAD

http://thefreethoughtproject.com/
category/cop-watch/police-brutality-cop-watch/

The image above depicts a citizen having a medical emergency who was pepper sprayed, tased, and drug from the car by a police officer. The citizens only offense was to be medically unable to respond to the officers commands to get out of the car.

For the Wolf the violent treatment of anyone he encounters, or has the opportunity to arrest is an everyday occurrence for him and he bears no remorse, nor does he have any inclination to change what he does. He is part of the 15 percent of police officers who will commit atrocities against citizens on a daily basis across the nation and then go home and sleep like a satiated wolf.

THE PROFESSIONAL

This officer only make up about 15% of the officers in any given police department. They are rare breed in today's' police departments. I am very proud to say that I have had the honor of working with and knowing a few men and women who fit this description. This police officer will address you as "sir" or "ma'am". They will follow protocol for whatever reason they pull you over. They will be courteous but firm. They are not there to be your friend, or your enemy. They already know that your heart is racing, and that more than likely you are not about to have the best day of your week. They will not mistreat your teenage child because most time they too have children that mean the world to them. They won't be moved by your agitation, or frustrated demonstrations. If they need to question you it will be handled in a professional manner. They may even explain to you that the truthful answer will make the situation flow more smoothly. *They are not pushovers, or soft if need be they can be as physical and as tough as the next officer* but they have learned that "the more your fight the more you write". So the peaceful solutions become the more sought after solution for these police officers. Their conversational approach to you is not inflammatory or insulting even if yours is.

This officer will try and stop one of his, or her colleagues from violating your constitutional rights. I once heard this said from one officer to another, *"This is as fucking blunt as I can put it. You are not getting me caught up in some bullshit law suit because you want to step on your own dick. You need to pull your shit together because I ain't lying for your ass."* This officer then snatched the citizens license from the hand of the WOLF, walked over to the citizen and returned it. He then said, *"I will go to war with you, I will fight for you, and I won't run off when the shit hits the fan but you better be right."* I was speechless but that was decades ago and in today's world I'm not sure that that speech is given anymore. Many times these officers are not popular as the two following examples will show.

The officer pictured below attempted to stop the abuse of a citizen by a fellow officer. And after 19 years on the job she was fired for stopping a chokehold from being applied to a handcuffed prisoner. This is the fear that good officers live with. If their department backs the aggressive violator he, or she will pay a heavy price for their interference. She lost her pension and all benefits for her 5 children despite evidence which verifies her side of the incident. She stood alone.

Freethoughtproject.com

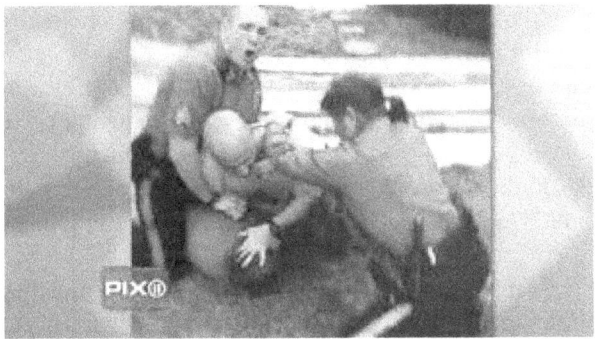

http://thefreethoughtproject.com/good-cop-punished-stepping-stop-fellow-cops-beating-mentally-ill-man/

Pictured above the 11 year veteran police officer above was fired for trying to stop 2 officers from beating a mentally ill man who was never arrested, or charged with a crime.

The professional officer commonly faces consequences like the two previous pictures. It is for this reason that 70 percent of the officers on the force do not make waves, or attempt to restrain their fellow officers when they cross the line. It is normal for a man to think of his wife and children and the obligations that he has as a provider.

The professional must weigh the consequences of his actions not only against how it affects his family but how much good will it do when most of the police department that he works for is in collusion with the renegade police officer. The officer pictured first who has 5 children stated that as she and her children have had to adjust to her life as a truck driver it has not been easy. One of her daughters will ask her why did she go to work that day.

The question that is avoided goes off like a bomb in every good cops head every day. *Why did you have to get involved, couldn't you have let it go.* Some officers say that they can't save everyone and they try and do all the good that they can. But to the one citizen that they chose not to save that statement rings very hollow. One young man told me that while he was being mistreated by one police officer he made eye contact with officer's partner who had chosen to just sit in the patrol car. The officer looked at him and just shook his head in disgust at his partner's actions.

The young man told me that he repeatedly looked to the other officer for help but none was given. But maybe the silent officer who did not get involved helped some old lady carry her groceries to her car later that day to make up for it. The second officer pictured was there to escort a compliant mental patient to a hospital. She called for backup in order to comply with department policies. When two sergeants arrived on the scene they immediately attacked the mental patient who was still compliant. Her efforts to pull them off cost her, her job as a police officer.

Such is the plight of many good officers who choose to protect and serve. Being alienated by their fellow officers, being declared liabilities by their own departments. Finally being eliminated for being too honest, and being tagged as unfit for duty because they refuse to lie, abuse, and kill like the rest of the Wolves, Curses, and Cowards.

Pictured below an officer buys lunch for a child who does not have enough money, it was his final act as a peace officer

Pictured above an officer buys shoes for a homeless man.

Two prior images show the undeniable humanity of police officers who are tasked with doing a tough job but who refuse to use it as an excuse to discard human decency. I applaud these officers and hope that officers like them across the nation will remain that way amid all the debris they have to make their way through just to get to the end of another shift. And I encourage them to find ways to speak out against the corrupt officers in their departments before it is too late. Because there is a rising tide of voices that will not go away or remain unheard in the face of citizens being abused and murdered by the very entity that was formed to protect them.

PEDESTRIAN CONTACT

This form of interaction with law enforcement is frequently experienced in larger metropolitan areas. Since pedestrian traffic is the major form of transport in the downtown areas of larger cities. In some areas police officers are assigned given areas of patrol that require walking. Of late this practice is becoming more frequent across the country due to the success that it is perceived to have had in jurisdictions where it has been applied. This contact allows the police officer to become more personally acquainted with the business owners, and residents who are common in the area. The preferred outcome is a bond that establishes a more open line of communication with the police men, and women who work the area.

Pedestrian contact can be made anywhere, as was recently noted in the Ferguson Missouri case which topped the news. This area was not a downtown street, or some commercial area this appeared to be a residential area in which a police officer made contact with man who wound up being shot to death as a result of attacking the officer through the window of his patrol vehicle. The race pimps took hold of the emotions of as many people as they could and stirred a fury against police officers across the country that is seldom scene. *No one waited for the autopsy report, or the official investigation to be completed.* Federal officials became embroiled in the investigation which was still incomplete. The officer had to resign from the police department prior to all the investigations being completed. Ultimately both the local and federal investigations cleared the officer and concluded that the officer was under attack while he was sitting in his patrol car. But *the people who make their living handing out victim cards had told so many lies that there was no room for the truth*. All this cannot be laid at the feet of the race baiters. For years the majority of the people who live in the community affected by aggressive officers have not been given a voice, have not been heard, have not been respected as citizens of this nation. And on a day when it appears that an officer actually did his job correctly the keg explodes anyway.

Several major police departments don't keep street-stop statistics, or don't release them. Chicago police refused to release numbers. Boston police say they don't keep the records. And the New Orleans police department isn't required to keep statistics on pedestrian stops.

In the city of New York stop, and frisk was used on over half a million people. The statistics note that 51% of the stops were used on black citizens, while Hispanic citizen garnered about 32% of the stops and Caucasian citizens attracted only 11% of the stop and frisk pat downs by the New York City Police Department. In one year some estimates put large cities at over a million pedestrian stops a year. *The necessity of evidence in a Terry Stop, or a stop and frisk is reasonable suspension which is less that the probable cause needed for an arrest.*

Officer the Supreme Court said a pat down from outside the clothing is for your safety. Are you asking to search me beyond that point? I am consenting to a pat down not an unwarranted search of my personal belongings.

The main purpose of a pedestrian stop or stop and frisk is to question an individual whom the officer believes to look suspicious, or out of place. In 1968 in the case of Terry vs. Ohio the Supreme Court said that police can do a search for weapons if they have a reasonable suspicion that the individual is armed, and dangerous. Notice the court only said for WEAPONS. That means no hands inside the pockets only a pat down from outside the garment. Too many times officers will play with wording in order to get you to agree to a search instead of a pat down. Or they will just violate your rights without saying anything. Also note the reasonable suspicion does not rise to the same level of evidence necessary to demonstrate *probable cause*, it pretty much just means *suspicion* which can be a bulge in your pocket or the outline of some object seen through your clothes. *It's not enough for an arrest but it is enough to warrant further investigation.*

A search without consent takes a higher level of suspicion, probable cause, or standing in order to be legal, whereas a "pat down" for safety takes far less legal evidence than the much more in depth search of your person by a peace officer.

With many officers the pat down is a tool that they use relentlessly. Since the measure of its legal application is really up to them and no one can measure their forthrightness. Baggy clothes which make it easy to conceal contraband are also an open door for suspicion regardless of any other action the citizen may or may not be involved in. Again officers will play with words to get your permission to go beyond a pat down with your unwary consent and it becomes a legal search instead of an illegal overstepping of bounds.

The conversation usually goes like this. OFFICER "Do you have any weapons *or anything* on you?" CITIZEN "No." OFFICER "I need to check you out for the safety of both of us because although you seem like a nice guy with *nothing to hide* it would be better if I did. I need you to turn around and put your hands on the wall for a *search*. At this point your cooperation opens the door for more than a cursory pat down. (The word *anything* may be replaced with *contraband*, *drugs*, or *anything illegal* which now means a joint or pills, methamphetamine, or any small object, or unidentified mass he chooses to pull out, or ask you to remove from your pockets.) If you began to protest the officer overstepping his bounds he will then want to know what are you hiding, and attempting to cast more suspicion on you for wanting to exercise your 4th amendment rights. If you attempt turn around or disengage from the officer during the search you are now guilty of resisting. *It all started with deceptive questions, or requests which the average citizen is unprepared for. It is what I call the game behind the game*.

This form of questioning, and request for consent takes the Supreme Court decision of 1968 beyond its original intent, and because you consented it becomes legal. You are guaranteed by the 5th amendment that you have the right not to self-incriminate in the interview process, or the court room. The 4th amendment secures your rights against unreasonable searches and seizures but once you consent you give permission for an open ended search which may go all the way to the tips of your toes. Backpacks which can be used to conceal weapons are normally included in the pat down for weapons. Remind the officer of the Terry Stop boundaries from 1968 stated for weapons because it was about the officers safety and not a violation of the 4th amendment.

Expect to be immediately on their bad side once you do but keep using the officer's name, and remain calm. Police officers do not always respond well to knowledgeable citizens. They do not like what they refer to as "YouTube lawyers" telling them how to do their jobs. This is true even if they are making an error, and especially if they are violating your rights on purpose. Your knowledge is now a threat to their egos. You may need to relate this information to appropriate persons later if a violation of your rights occurs, and it will look better if you kept your cool and did not antagonize the police officer.

One frequently used set of questions are "am I being detained?" "Am I suspected of committing a crime?" "What crime am I suspected of committing?" "Am I free to go?"

If the officer refuses to answer the questions he is up to something or he is angry and is hoping to anger you so that he can bait you into an giving him a reason to arrest you. Do not physically resist you will have a time and place to address the officer's actions where you will be safe from his baton, taser, and gun.

I noted earlier that the Supreme Court advised that if a traffic stop is initiated due to a violation the officer does not have grounds to detain you for a canine officer to come and do a walk around. The traffic stop should terminate as soon as he finishes writing the citation and the completion of the task should not take an exorbitant amount of time. *It will be interesting to see how this new ruling affects detaining pedestrians.* Unless some other form of evidence, or probable cause exist then you as a citizen should clarify what you mean before you consent.

Some officers will just tell you to turn around or raise your hands and start to search you. Ask them are they looking for weapons, and state the Supreme Court says a pat down is passing your hands against my clothing from the outside not going through my wallet, phone, or pockets. If the officer feels something he cannot recognize and asks you what it is, or asks you to turn out your pockets. You should ask him if he felt a weapon and if so what kind of weapon. A folded piece of paper in your pocket is not evidence of a crime. *Your personal belongings do not have to be made privy to a Terry Stop pat down.*

The feel of a 9mm or a revolver or an illegal knife does not feel like a wad of paper or a wallet.

If an officer pushes with his words for you to submit to a search that is illegal you may submit but be very clear it that is against your rights as a citizen, and for the record you do so under duress of unlawful arrest. This can help you later should you need to defend yourself in court. If the officer has some information that you are not privy to it may make his request legal despite the seemingly far reaching latitude of his requests, or commands.

71

Learn the boundaries of the Terry Stop, know the boundaries and be able to respectfully relate them. The officer will not like it because of ego driven self-image problems. But you may cause the police officer to cut short his, or her intended illegal treatment of you the citizen. Again, if the officer persists you have other recourses available to you after the incident is over. Do not fight the officer physically unless you know that they mean to hurt, or kill you.

PHYSICAL CONTACT WITH THE POLICE

On occasion you may be approached by more than one officer. If they are working as a team one may stand behind while the officer in front you conducts the interview. *If you lay one hand on a police officer you are in violation of the law in most states.* If the police officer believes that it has become necessary for you to be taken down the officer behind you has been trained to take you off your feet. I will not divulge the tactics used for the safety of officers who may need to use these techniques in the performance of their duties. If you are taken down, and a pain compliance technique is being used the officers are trained to ease up on the pain when you comply. Too frequently this does not happen due to the fact that officers are human, and adrenaline is flowing and they may not realize how much force is being used, or they want to teach you a lesson for resisting, or sadly they may not have enough training in pain compliance techniques, and then there are those who do not care and just want to hurt someone.

The training of police officers in these areas frequently does not include recognizing, and monitoring his, or her levels of excitement, or engagement.

Believe it or not this is why on occasion after a vehicle, or foot chase you will see a fleeing suspect down on the ground, or in a position of surrender, and an officer will just level him and maybe even throw punches, and knees at the subdued subject. *If the officer is repeating the phrase stop resisting over, and over and you are not resisting you should yell "I am not resisting" (use the officers name like I instructed you to earlier if you have it)* continue making the statement "I am not resisting"

Remember that the police officer is wound up and more than likely it was triggered by the introduction of physical contact, there are times however when the police officers triggers have nothing to do with you, but are entirely his own as his personal demons have him acting out. That officer may not be in control of his faculties. You are at their mercy if there are multiple police officers involved the probability of one of them stopping the others is minuscule. You should note this before becoming resistant to the officer. You should be able to note whether the officer is agitated or not just a few seconds into the contact.

I fractured another officer's wrist just practicing because I was wound up, and honestly I did not know my own strength, and I knew of his martial arts prowess, and I was determined not to get my butt beat that day. So as his intensity ratcheted up so did mine. Combat is intense, full force, no hesitation contact in its most brute form. This is where citizens get hurt. But in most cases it is up to the citizen to run, or comply, or fight. Their level of resistance to not comply, or argue with a police officer can be the most mitigating factor in what happens.

There are those cases that do not follow any hard, and fast rules of conduct on the part of a peace officer when a citizen is going to be mistreated no matter what they do. *I know beforehand what I am willing to do*, and the consequences of that they may bring. I have thought it out, and given instructions to my family regarding what I want done in the event that I am forced to make certain choices.

 I can take verbal abuse, unlawful detainment, even illegal searches because there are avenues to address each of these after I survive. But if an officer is demonstrating a physically aggressive posture, glaring in a threatening manner, hand on gun while talking to me while I'm compliant and nonthreatening, verbally aggressive toward me but does not call for back up then these become things that I must weigh before allowing myself to be handcuffed and made defenseless so to speak. I have to consider are we in an isolated area? Is it after dark? Is this police officer a Wolf with a badge.

You as a citizen must weigh out your own comfort, and trust levels. *Do not ever think that being angry is combat style it is not and it never will be. Policemen kill angry people all the time.* If you are not practiced, and competent, and able to relate your reason for non-compliance in a court of law, and then take whatever penalty that may come forth you should fully comply, and avoid arguing no matter what you are feeling.

The average citizen cannot even remember the last time they were in a combat situation, and they are not generally prepared. I see people screaming over, and over again once the police have put their hands on them because they are not ready for that level of engagement. But by then it is too late. The citizen fails to realize that they are not in a barber shop argument, they are on the street and the pepper spray, asp, taser, and gun on the police officers side are real, and at his, or her disposal.

I am going to punch you in the head and demand
that you put your hands behind your back while
I keep hitting you in the face even though you are totally defenseless.

I will repeat that the training of police officers in these areas frequently does not include recognizing, and monitoring his, or her own levels of excitement, or engagement. I cannot count the number of times I have heard officers yelling "calm down" while

This form of resistance is done out of fear, and pain. It may be interpreted as disregard of the law but it is not.

snatching a citizen's arm, or wrist to the most extreme angles just short of breaking them. If the citizen believes the only thing keeping their wrists or elbows from snapping is the resistance that they are applying to counter the possibility of being seriously injured they will not comply. *This form of resistance is done out of fear, and pain. It may be interpreted as disregard of the law but it is not.* In that moment two things are going on.

The officer is either out of control, or trying to hurt the citizen, or the citizen is in fight, or flight mode. *Fight or flight is a survival mode* where a person feels they are facing a life, or death situation and no amount of yelling calm down, or quit resisting will get through to them immediately. *Their intellect is switched off and a much more primal instinct has taken over.* It is likely that they won't remember half of the things that occurred, and it is not probable that the citizen will be able to intelligently discern, and follow an officer's commands as they are yelled into their ears from 6 inches away. The volume only serves to rattle the senses even more.

I have seen men with clearly broken arms, and broken hands fighting as if they could not feel the pain of the injury. One such fellow told me "It was fight or die, and I did not want to die."
Most police officers have never stopped to consider how a citizen who has been mased, and has three people hitting him in the head, face, legs, and back can rationally comply with a command not to cover his, or her face, and to put their hands behind their back literally opening themselves up to more punches, and elbows without any protection.

The average officer feels like the citizen bought it on themselves, so all professionalism goes out the window, and if there are multiple officers involved then the mob mentality takes over and there is no conscious awareness in a mob. Rodney King proves that.

Survive Police Contact

I repeat this section for the police officers who will read this and see themselves, and or their colleagues who are guilty of railroading citizens that they hurt, and then file charges for resisting arrest.

A police officer can worsen the situation when they apply too much pain on a citizen by way of a pain compliance hold. The citizen may have been resisting, but now the citizen is frightened of serious injury and cannot comply. So resisting arrest charges, and or assault of a peace officer charges are filed, but were unnecessarily bought on by poor training, or abuse. **When the officer is hurting a citizen, and yelling at the citizen to stop resisting from 6 inches away from their ear this brings confusion to the mind of a citizen not trained in intense combat techniques.** *The officer should lower his tone to a calm level, and ask for compliance. "When you comply, I will ease up on the pain." It's that simple.*

Freethoughtproject.com
The man above is following orders and surrendering but an out of control officer kicks him in the head anyway rendering him unconscious.

Having watched the video the other officer in the video did not make any attempt to restrain, or discourage his partner from any continued aggression. His failure to act does not exempt him in any manner because once the rogue police officer breaks the law right in front of you he is a criminal with the one exception of wearing a uniform.

77

The same officer would not dream of standing by and allowing an ordinary citizen to brutally kick another citizen into unconsciousness with a boot to the side of the head, but he will look the other way if a fellow police officer does it.

In refusing to do his sworn duty he puts himself into the same boat as the abusive police officer. What law prohibits him from arresting the officer for assault with bodily injury?

Taking the criminals weapon, cuffing him, and taking him in like any other criminal. The officer instead chooses to become party to a civil lawsuit for not fulfilling his oath of office and allowing a defenseless citizen to be brutalized. Only one officer was charged in this incident.

If you are given a command to comply do so without becoming physically resistant. Once the interaction becomes physical unless you are a trained fighter you are putting your life at risk. You may have to disarm, render unconscious, or kill the officer prior to the arrival of back up if he has called for it. Back up may show up even without the officer calling. When they arrive they do not come to sort things out. They generally come to do whatever the initial officer says needs to be done.

Should you believe your life is on the line the first law of nature is self-preservation. You should not make a rash decision, be certain of your situation. Whether you win, or lose you will in most cases end up in court facing a judge, and jury.

 The previous statement applies only if you survive the conflict if it moves into a deadly force situation you may be forced to do something you could never see coming.

By complying and making it known that it is under protest you are establishing grounds for a solid complaint, or law suit. Officers do not want to be sued, or have write ups in their personnel files. We will cover this area in a later chapter. For now just remember *the citizen needs to state that they are not freely consenting to the unconstitutional search but under threat of unlawful imprisonment they are forced to submit.*

I know that it is a mouth full but the citizen must establish that their compliance does not mean that they are freely consenting. Further note that the officer may appear angry at your exercising your constitutional rights. He will perceive it as a challenge to his power, or authority. The officer may grab you or put his hands in your face and began cursing or yelling at you.

 If you touch him it becomes assault against a peace officer and the situation now ratchets up to a physical confrontation. These men and women have been trained to believe that they are "the law" instead of functioning as if they are here to "uphold the law".

So they feel that whatever they say goes and that they can do whatever they want and you should not question it. That is why you must be prepared and know that to exercise your rights as a citizen will be taken personally, and may evoke an even more aggressive demeanor from this misguided public servant.

The officer may call for backup. Do not wait on backup before you comply. Remember a backup police officers only purpose is to back up their fellow officer. They are not coming to decide who is right or wrong. You should be firm but be as respectful as possible. Defiant words, and profanity only adds fuel to the fire.

You cannot win a fight on the street with your sharp angry words. Use your head and win this battle where it really matters. You cannot take this officers job on the street, nor can you get him fired on the street. This happens in a much different setting where his baton, mace, taser and gun are but accoutrements on his uniform.

FALSE REPORTS

Never attempt to lie on an officer it can bring much more serious charges. In addition to that once you have been identified as a prevaricator any other charges you level against a law enforcement official may be categorized as fictitious even if it really happened.

Many police officers are walking, and breathing lie detectors capable of sniffing out falsehoods in a nanosecond.

Policemen get lied to every day and they learn to read cues that a citizen gives off without even knowing it. This is also one of the reasons that police officers have such an edge on them. I can see it in their eyes when their minds shift to the officer mentality.

A hardness comes over their expressions as their facial muscles tense and change. Many officers have had a lifetime of negative interactions due to the nature of their jobs, and bad attitudes. One of the more distasteful aspects of the job is not just being reported but being wrongfully reported, or lied on.
Note the young woman in the following picture.

The photo below shows a young woman putting her phone into her bra, once inside the police station she requested to use the restroom where she made a phone call to ask a friend how to get the policeman in trouble. She was advised to say he molested her. The entire incident was recorded by the officer's lapel camera and her false report failed.

The photo exposes a glaring mistake the officer made as he conducts a field interview with the suspected drunk driver. He does not keep track of her hands and what she was doing. Had that been a derringer, or a small can of mace he would already be behind in his reaction time. Maybe he saw what she was doing but forgot about the phone being in her bra. He did follow two very important protocols that evening, he did not search a female alone on the street and he kept his lapel camera on. So her desire for vengeance fell flat. Sometimes citizens will make false accusations and have friends back them up. ***But a far more damaging form of reporting now exists. This new type of reporting does not get put down on and affidavit at the police station or recorded by internal affairs.*** This report goes out to the entire world at large and judgment can be swift and vengeful and misdirected. One which can end careers even when the officer has done nothing outside the bounds of the law, or department policies.

A newer form of false reporting has begun occurring across the country as media outlets, websites, and sometimes the members of the public at large will release clips of incidents which portray the police officer in a negative light. The media outlets, and talk venues want to be the first out with the hottest news. Radio stations have their own internet sights on which to post material for the discussion of today's hottest topics, and controversial news. The average citizen can upload to Facebook, YouTube, or Twitter and have a video go viral in a matter of hours. These videos may be edited, or unedited videos as well as audio exchanges which can be viewed, or listened to in, or out of context. Most often these releases only serve to stoke the fires of anger toward police officers who may at times be doing their jobs correctly.

These forms of sensationalism can sway public opinion before an officer is ever given an impartial hearing. The pundits come out asking that the officer's job, and career be forfeited, along with his freedom. The citizen is deified and put on a pedestal as an example of police brutality no matter the circumstances of the incidents. The information released is not an official complaint, or accusation but it can be far more damaging to the image of the police departments across the nation, and around the world. Once these images, and videos reach the viral status in the matter of a day or two whatever misinformation that it carries becomes the truth of the day. Now other news portals regurgitate the same error filled reports, and soon there are embellishments being made to the story that will never be completely uprooted.

The young lady pictured previously was arrested for DWI and she was not searched by the male officer who administered a field sobriety test. The young woman failed the test. During the interaction she placed her phone into her bra as can be seen in still photo taken from the video feed. The young woman was transported without being searched by the male officer. After she reached the police station she asked to be excused to the restroom where she began calling, and soliciting advice on how to get the police officer into trouble.

The advice she was given was to lie on him and say that he touched her inappropriately in the back of his squad car. The officer heard her talking on her phone in the restroom and interrupted the conversation at which time the young lady began making the accusations she had been told to make. The police officers lapel camera had recorded the entire interaction and it saved him from a career ending episode. Close calls like these happen all the time and in some cases good officers lose their jobs and careers.

The officer leaves this interaction either thinking to himself keep the lapel camera on at every traffic stop, or those people are lying sacks of excrement, and they don't deserve any respect from me. They would ruin me in a heartbeat and then brag about it to their friends while my family goes hungry. I will show them. This happens far more frequently than the public gets wind of. Now think about the attitude of the officer when he goes out to serve the public again? Does he have a chip on his shoulder? Is he overly harsh with his words? Will he let the next drunk female go in order to avoid a second complaint. Complaints stay in an officer's file permanently. What if his next evaluator is a female supervisor? How does he tell his wife, or girlfriend why he is home on paid leave until all this is sorted out. All these play into his decision making. And the key to the tainted officers attitude can be found in a citizen with a bad attitude who is looking to hurt the officer for doing his job.

It is at this point that the antagonists' who make their living stirring the cauldron of offence, and discontentment behind these kinds of incidents open the door for a much more destructive rhetoric. The information in these situations has been skewed in order to prove some socio/political point. It is not infrequent that some protest leaders make behind the scene deals with the city administration, or the police department in which they get lucrative contracts teaching cultural sensitivity to the department's upper echelon of leadership. After which they ratchet down the protest, take their loot and, leave until the next opportunity presents itself.

On the other side of side of this same issue law enforcement information has been used, or withheld with the intent to cover for officers who have crossed the line, or because an investigation is still underway and no official stance can be taken until everything is complete. Frequently the information provided to the public is to further an agenda that has nothing to do with revealing the truth.

The media across the north Texas area covered the incident below as an example of police abuse because the suspect was unarmed. After the complete video was released it became apparent that the officer had followed every protocol in his efforts to affect an arrest without undue violence

freethoughtproject.com

After evading the police near the scene of a burglary at the end of a high speed chase this man was told to stop over 20 times as he attempts to overtake the officer while saying "kill me". The media tried to turn the incident into a racially motivated execution.

The release of the entire video completely silenced all calls for the officer to be fired, and prosecuted. The public was in an uproar and untrained assumptions were abundant. The officer of course was on administrative leave, his family was probably afraid for him more than ever before, he would have undoubtedly been afraid for the safety of his family. This fear would be based on the rhetoric coming from some quarters which state that if our families are not off limits then neither are the families of law enforcement officers.

The desire for immediate answers places heavy demands on police departments to release information, and take action on incomplete information. When police departments follow professional investigative standards they are frequently accused of engineering a cover up for the benefit of the officer, or officers involved in whatever the incident may have been.

A proper investigation generally does not allow for the release of any information until the investigation is complete. This will also include time for the District Attorney to make a decision regarding prosecution, or whether to take the evidence before a grand jury, and allow the citizens to decide if there is enough evidence to indict the police officer. All these legal actions require time, and unfortunately this delay gives a platform to the entities, and people who have agendas that run counter to finding, and revealing the truth.

Recently I observed an officer fired publicly by the chief of police in order to avoid a backlash when the officer shot and killed an unarmed man who was coming toward him and would not stop when ordered to get on the floor. The rookie officer had not followed a safer approach that was being coordinated by his training officer and in doing so he helped bring about a shooting situation that may have been avoided with more officers involved in subduing the suspect. There was no criminal law violation but there was clearly bad judgment on the part of the officer. The Chief of Police was clearly trying to avoid backlash with his hasty decision. Police unions, and organizations in the area severely rebuked, and chastised the Chief of Police for his actions which were considered hasty. They also referred to the "administrative investigation" as incomplete, and unfair to the officer, his family and the police officers under his command. One sympathizer said that the officers face, and name are plastered all over the internet and it is likely that he will never work as a police officer again. It is clear that the whole thing was done as a show of support to the very vocal groups that have protested repeatedly across the country where the use of deadly force against minorities is staggering.

HOW TO FILE A COMPLAINT

Laws, and regulations regarding filing complaints against police officials vary from state to state. I will give a few guidelines which will be helpful in which ever state you reside. Use the internet to search for the reporting requirements in your state.

First your attitude and demeanor will go a long way in determining how seriously your complaint is taken. Frequently after a negative interaction the citizen is left feeling powerless, dehumanized, and violated. This can lend itself to some serious emotional responses on the part of the victimized citizen. These emotions have gotten the best of many citizens with justifiable complaints, causing them to lose the only battle a citizen can win against a bad officer. Being offended is one of the hardest emotions to handle for some people, so a game plan on what steps you need to take will be a necessity in order to do well in the next phase of your encounter with law enforcement.

Make up your mind how far you are willing to go in the process. It may be as simple as going into the police station and filling a written report, or contacting the District Attorney's office for your city, or county, maybe even reaching out to the Justice Department. Whatever may be your level of resolve you must be willing walk away from the entire process knowing that you have done your part as a citizen. *Accept up front that not all instances of officers stepping across the line, and abusing, or suppressing the rights of citizens will result in the officer being disciplined for their infraction.* In most cases citizen complaints are recorded in an officer's file, and notations are given as to whether the complaint was founded, or unfounded. *This has a two pronged effect. When the officer comes up for promotion, or review the complaint will be seen by the officer's superiors. Secondly if the same complaint presents itself over, and over even if the officer has not been disciplined, or found to be guilty of the infraction the complaints become a cause of concern to any supervisor worth their salt.* Or the complaints may become evidence for a legal proceeding down the road should the officer's abusive ways lead them being indicted on criminal charges.

> *"If you don't get reported once a month you ain't doing it right."*

These were and still are the words of too many training officers as they acclimate their trainees to life in the police force. *In other words don't worry about citizen's complaints, they don't amount to anything.* That is what I refer to as the Blue Kool Aid. Officers who have no fear of accountability will have no regard for the citizens, or the constitutional rights of the citizens they serve. When you are a 21 year old rookie fresh out of the academy and you are on probation you don't question the man holding the clipboard and doing his evaluations for the week.

"You do as you are told."

The necessary skills to maneuver currents like these do not normally exist in the repertoire of rookies. So they comply and drink the blue kook aid.

The police lawsuit statistics in this country are eye opening. *Since 2009 the city of New York paid a 500,000,000 that's right half a billion dollars in law suits stemming from wrongful arrests, and civil rights violations.* The city of Philadelphia has paid 40 million dollars from its coffers to deal with 584 of the 1200 lawsuits filed against the city since 2009. There are about one and half million people in the city of Philadelphia.

The recent uprising in Baltimore, Maryland falls in line with the 11,500,000 spent on legal fees and settlements against the city in recent years. The Chicago Sun times has reported that the *City of Chicago has paid out half a billion dollars in settlements over the past decade that averages 50 million a year.* There are many figures available which would astound you but suffice it to say that Cities lose billions of dollars due to negligence and abuse claims.

The most devastating aspect of the abuse and negligence cost is that the billions of dollars in costs come from the hard working citizens of the communities in which the offending officers work. The officers themselves, and the departments do not bear any of the financial responsibility for the officer's actions. Issues like these are becoming more, and more politicized as calls are being made to nationalize the police departments across the nation.

The training of Police Officers and the guidelines by which they conduct themselves are becoming hot button topics in political circles, as well as serving to polarize citizens along racial boundaries. Race baiters on both sides have sprung into action and applied their crafts in order to come out ahead financially on the suffering of others. And you the citizen are now burdened with deciphering the intent of people who will contact you in an attempt to come to your aid, as well as those who would exploit you for their own personal gain. It is interesting to note that abuses occur across racial lines. They occur more frequently in minority communities but are not exclusive to such communities. One does not have to look far to find Caucasian men and women physically abused by police officers.

As you go through the process of reporting an officer be prepared by familiarizing yourself with as much knowledge of the processes as you can. Knowing what the requirements are in your city, and county can prepare you to be successful. Knowing the next step to take in case you are met with an obstacle can be very comforting as you navigate the system and go through the process.

Some states give discretionary authority to local prosecutors in determining if the grand jury will even hear the evidence if there is a case to be filed. Some complaints are handled in house with the local police department where there have been violations of departmental policies when cases do not show any violation of legal statutes.

A recent case of an officer being fired for violating department policy after the shooting to death a young man who had driven his vehicle through the glass window of a dealership and was coming at the police officer, and would not comply with the officers commands to get on the ground. *The officer did not violate any state statute in the shooting, but he did violate department policies so he was terminated prior to any official investigation being concluded. This was determined by what is known as an Administrative Investigation.* This is very rare in law enforcement circles and it will cause a great deal of upheaval in the department as officers receive the message that their Chief of Police will act according to his conscious, or political pressure against his own department. Whatever the Chief of Police's reasons were he was within his rights just, as the police officer who rushed in to confront the suspect, and bypassed his training officer, and other peers who were concocting a plan of attack was within his rights as a police officer to do so. *Everything that is legal is not fair.* But at least the officer gets to walk away with his life.

The same standards that apply to any criminal case are the standards that apply to an officer's violations of your rights as a citizen. There has to be enough evidence to rise to the level of being beyond a reasonable doubt in the eyes of the District Attorney, and invariably the grand jury. In the case of the District Attorney this is where the discretionary power comes in.

Beyond reasonable doubt generally means enough evidence so as to point to the quilt of the accused once all available evidence is weighed.

Without this preponderance of evidence cases are usually dismissed. When it comes down to your word against the officers it can be very frustrating because it is very likely that the investigation could stall. In those instances a polygraph exam may be offered, or requested either by you, or the police investigators. Although not acceptable as evidence in court the polygraph can go a long way toward establishing credibility for you the citizen, or vindicating the officer.

On occasion we have heard for calls for the Justice Department to step in where it appears that discrepancies exist in the process of achieving a justice, and a fair end to cases of official misconduct. The state in which you reside has an Attorney General's office which can be called in to review the findings of your local district attorney, or in some cases have oversight of the process. This may be an alternative when the local District Attorney has interests, other than that of justice, or when blatant issues present themselves such as evidence of favoritism, and, wrong doing on the part of the District Attorney's Office.
The relationship of police departments with District Attorneys, and Judges can leave the general public feeling like they are standing on the outside looking in. Earlier in the book I recalled a story of receiving a citation, and asking my son who he thought the Judge would believe when I set it for court. We both sadly agreed that the average citizen's word does not carry the weight of a sworn officer in the judicial system, and thus the sense of powerlessness that the citizen feels on the street is carried over to the court room due to the lack of impartiality of court room officials. Having observed court proceedings over, and over it is the rare occasion that a citizen's testimony alone without any supporting evidence is given much weight when the testimony of a sworn peace officer is in direct opposition to it. Police officers know this and it only adds to their insensitivity. In each case of mistaken identity, or convictions of innocent citizens it is not the court that lies, or hides evidence it is the police, or the District Attorney who commit these life altering atrocities upon the citizens. As is made evident by Project Innocence. The guilt that falls on the judicial system is that they turn a blind, or prejudicial eye to the fates of too many defendants who are being railroaded.

Seldom are there consequences to the negligent, or heinous actions of detectives, or District Attorneys who hide or ignore evidence that would exonerate innocent citizens. I find it most appalling that there is no discussion of pursuing charges against a clearly crooked prosecutor, or policeman who fabricates evidence against a citizen. The citizen may be later let out of prison and given some monetary compensation but by and large the true law breaker walks away with a pension and a full and happy life.

The US Justice Department has evidence of scores of innocent people in prison but will not tell them they are innocent of any crime.

http://thefreethoughtproject.com/60-prisoners-north-carolina-declared-innocent-jail/

Even though there are clearly violations of ethics and possible criminal malfeasance no one is prosecuted, or fired but it is the citizen who through higher taxes that pays the cost for the injured parties grief. The bottom line is that evidence is sometimes suppressed which would exonerate the accused but police, and prosecutors, and even the Justice department will withhold it in order to get a conviction.

As mentioned previously there have been agreements made between the police, and prosecutors, and judges in some cases that predispose the court to levy heavier fines, and penalties on accused perpetrators prior to their ever entering a courtroom, and taking an oath to tell the truth and nothing but the truth. The court has in essence said that it does not matter what you say, we don't want to hear you.

Here is a tip, look for any unexplained stray marks on any citations you receive. These have been used as communication methods to let the court know who needs to be taught a lesson. But what happens if the officer who is writing the citation is being less than honorable? Sadly with the courts, and the District Attorney's office in collusion with the street officer the voice of the citizen is muted, and the public is victimized.

http://thefreethoughtproject.com/judge-quits-speeding-ticket-quotas-blows-whistle/#f5dfs5GsFuDt2QUp.01

The judge above blows the whistle on ticket scams that have gone on with the prosecutor, the courts and the police for years.

Who then has oversight to right the wrong? This is why the reporting process is so necessary for the average citizens. I believe it is in this process that we are most powerful. When each citizen fulfills their duty to report, follow up, and hold accountable those in power to serve us we will win the day. The abuse of citizens is cross cultural. There are more severe atrocities on certain citizens but overall every race of citizen in this country has experienced some heinous interaction with the police. We have all felt the sting of hopelessness as another official who is tasked with protecting us turns and becomes our worst nightmare.

What should a citizen expect when filing a complaint against a law enforcement officer? Expect to be scrutinized heavily. Frequently people with axes to grind come into a police station for revenge. Old girlfriends, or boyfriends will file complaints of misconduct, harassment, violations of the law etc... These are attempts to get even with an officer for personal matters due to unhappy partings. Most departments are well aware that many police officers use their positions as authority figures to acquire favors from what are known as "uniform freaks". Although discouraged departmentally there are no real punishments for an officer having a one night stand with another person and then choosing not to call them back, or return their calls. It is a sign of low moral fiber, and possibly a peek into how this officer will use future power, and authority but it does not constitute an infraction of any statute of law, or departmental policy. Most police departments have "Moral Turpitude" clauses in an officer's contract, however it is rarely if ever used due to the lowering of standards in the communities of our nation.

The officers tasked with investigating other police officers can at times be somewhat aggressive in finding the "reason" you are coming into the police station, rather than focusing on the abuse, or negligence of their fellow police officer. *Tell them you were really concerned about the matter. Do not discuss your anger over the situation with them. Nor should you go into an "I demand justice" tirade. The time to become emotionally moved is in front of the news cameras where it can do the most damage.*

Expect to be identified, and probably have your information run for a criminal back ground check as well as a check for any outstanding warrants you may have. Unfortunately, some people have shown up and filed the complaint only to be arrested right there on some other charge. Make sure that your business is taken care of. Never call in to the police department to report a police officer. That is as useless as an umbrella in a rockslide.

Do not give an officer on the street your phone number with a promise that a supervisor will call you back even if the officer is the supervisor.

Your phone call into the police station to report an officer will probably go no further than the desk you called it in to. If you do call get a name, and ask to set an appointment to come in and talk to whoever is tasked with investigating officer misconduct. Also be sure to ask for a call back verifying that the appointment has been noted. Some departments will try and wear you down by forgetting the appointment, or getting busy, or placing the officer on a call when you show up. *Write down who you spoke with, and their rank and time of day, or night. In some states it is not a crime to record a phone conversation without telling the party on the other end of the phone call as long as you are a participant in the call and not just eaves dropping.* If you wish you may advise whoever answers the phone when you call the police station that you will be recording the conversation for your records. If they protest ask is it department policy, or are they making it up as they go. Most police departments record your phone contact but they never advise you up front that they are doing so.

Do not ask for a supervisor to come to the scene, and then tell on the officer. Most supervisors are going to side with their men, or try and pacify you so that the complaint will not go any further. This is usually done by trying to explain the officer's actions, or by assuring you that they would handle the situation with the officer personally. *At times the supervisor will even accuse you of being the problem. Some supervisors will take an inordinate amount of time getting to the scene hoping that you will give up and go home, thus saving them paper work and keeping them out of the middle of a lawsuit.*

All policemen want you to comply with their every command. Most policemen take it personally, and are irritated when a citizen refuses to comply. Even if it is within the citizen's constitutional right to do so. As I said earlier it is at this point that creative thinking comes into play as way of the police officer getting what he wants from you. And of course for the less creative officer there is always brute force, and false allegations, baiting the citizen and arrest.

"You may beat the rap but you won't beat the ride." The RAP is the arrest charges, the RIDE is the trip to jail, and your car towed at your expense. As well as the inconvenience, and cost to you to get out of jail.

And in the mind of the police officer any misfortune that befalls you is no skin of his nose it's all your fault, or tough luck. If the police supervisor meets you on the scene he may ask for your call back information. In the past this has been done only to call you back later and say that the appropriate action was taken but because of privacy matters related to personnel files the action taken cannot be discussed with outside personnel. This happens too frequently. Look for signs that the supervisor may seem overly concerned, or disinterested because usually after you leave the scene conversation never happened, and your attempt at registering a complaint has been wasted if you have not put a complaint in writing or scheduled an appointment time.

Never attempt to complain on an officer to a supervisor on the street. Always go into the Police Station.

The proper steps must be followed in order to save someone else from going through what you went through or worse.

I frequently wonder if the last person I heard about on the news who was abused or killed by a wolf in uniform could have been saved if the citizens who were abused last year, or last month, or last week had just said something. I ponder what would have been the outcome if the officers in that police department cared about citizen safety at all, or had chosen to say something?

You should take a trusted friend with you to the appointment as a witness. I recommend setting your smart phone, or digital recorder to record the conversation. As I said earlier you should check your state statutes regarding recording a private conversation without notifying the other party. In some states it is perfectly legal and admissible in court. Check first. Or you can just let the investigating officer know that you will be recording the interaction for precautionary reasons. No need to explain any further.

Since you will be required to give a written statement go ahead and write it out at home before you leave for the police station. You can transcribe the statement onto department complaint forms if necessary once you arrive at the station. You can rewrite, and add elements of the interaction at home without feeling rushed or intimidated for changing your story when in fact your memory recall is working like any normal person. It is important to remember no name calling, or angry statements just stick to the facts.

You should expect to have to tell your side of the story more than a few times. This is done to see if your change your story. The officer may interrupt you in an attempt to see if your story changes by asking questions. The officer may also manifest a disbelieving mannerism regarding your complaint. Do not let this attitude shake you. You may still be emotional about the incident. If this is the case you can ask for a break, and try pulling yourself together. Better to call a time out and gather your thoughts than to allow the continued abuse of another citizen, because there will be a next one. The abusive officer is not going to stop with you unless something changes and you have the power to force that change. As I suggested earlier a good friend who can accompany you to be of moral support as you go through the process may be helpful in this time.

Never give a verbal complaint to a supervisor, internal affairs investigator, or desk sergeant. Always insist on writing it down. If you have taken the time to write out your grievance prior to coming to the police station as suggested you may forward the grievance to a city council member, the Chief of the police department, an investigative journalist, or another community leader The more attention you can muster to your complaint the harder it will be to bury it. If you do mail the complaint to a department official send it as certified mail so that there is a record of its receipt and who signed for it. Include your contact information so that any questions they have can be directly relayed to you. Let them know that your contact with them is not official at this point but that you want to keep them in the loop while you are going through this process within the police department.

Use the officer's name as a heading at the top of the page and follow it up with a charge such as:

Abuse of Power	**Excessive Use of Force**
Cruelty	**Sexual Harassment**
Civil Rights Violations	**Intimidating a Witness**
Assault	**Psychological Abuse**
Illegal Search and Seizure	**Discrimination**
Unlawful Detention	**Official Oppression**
Intimidation and Coercion	**Torture**
Official Misconduct	**Harassment**

Make it clear in your first sentence that you are requesting an official, not informal, but official investigation into the actions of the police officer. If the incident is traffic related make an official public information request on the number of traffic stops the officer has made and the demographics of such data. Ask for discipline information related to this officer. Request that any dash cam footage of the incident be saved and if possible released to you the citizen. Ask has he, or she been transferred, and if so how frequently. These are all questions that your attorney can get for your case if this incident needs to be taken to court. You as a citizen are trying to get as much traction, and momentum started on your complaint as possible, and these types of request will attract the attention necessary to keep your complaint from being filed away, and forgotten. This may cost you some money in copy fees but it demonstrates the seriousness of your intent to follow through in this situation, and it keeps those responsible for the investigation on their toes.

Do not just call back and leave messages, or ask how the investigation is going but instead send certified letters asking for a written response, or send emails with a read receipt attachment.

If you have a witness, have them write statements as well that can corroborate your claims of officer misconduct. It may not be necessary for your witnesses to appear with you initially. However they will need to be interviewed regarding what they saw, or heard. Be aware that just as there are statutes of limitations on criminal cases there are usually time limitations on reporting a peace officer's misconduct. These time restraints differ according to the type of violations that occurred as well as the jurisdictions as set forth in department policies, and the statutes that govern the area of occurrence.

If you have some evidence do not pass it around to your brother in law, cousin, or neighbor like some show and tell article. In the police department it is called a "chain of evidence" it keeps up with who has handled the evidence as a way of protecting it from tampering, or contamination. Keep it in a secure location, a safety deposit box or personal safe would be my suggestions. If the police investigators ask for it make it available but video yourself handing it over and get a receipt to protect against it being lost. If it is something that can be duplicated then do so. See if the investigator will take a copy of the evidence in lieu of the original. If not at least you will have a duplicate of the evidence.

One recent case comes to mind in which an officer was caught because evidence of the victims bodily secretions were found on his night stick, flash light, steering wheel, and gear selector in his patrol car. The officer violated the victim with his hand. Again I ask what if the victim had kept quiet and said nothing? How far would the officer have gone with the next helpless woman he came into contact with? How many times has he already done this or worse? Did the fear of other victims allow him to continue on doing this to it to other citizens? And for how long?

It is our responsibility to say something for the sakes of our sons, and daughters. And the sons and daughters of our friends and neighbors.

Once you have formally filed your complaint a determination must be made by the receiving officer as to the seriousness of the complaint. Once again make certain to write the most serious claim at the top of the form with the officer's name. a As the complaint is reviewed initially it will be categorized and the subsequent investigation if any will be based on this determination.

Some citizens complain that their complaint is being unfairly downgraded. When this happens if you have written a clear description of the incident and feel that it has been unfairly evaluated you have other options. The officials that were mentioned earlier such as the Chief of the Police Department, the city council member, the community leader, the City Attorney, District Attorney, or the investigative journalist for local media may become good resources. Your agenda at this point is to get as much traction on your complaint as possible.

Now if your complaints are over the top and unbelievable such as the officer ran over 3 children and then shot up the neighborhood grocery store before driving off. You will be considered a mental case, and your allegations will be pushed aside. If you have made farfetched allegations before, or have a history of unfounded allegations then any new allegations you make could be looked at as suspect even if they are grounded, thus making it harder to prove.

Trivial complaints such as the officer changed lanes without signaling, or the officer cut me off can be investigated but these are not complaints that significantly affect the ability of the police department to run effectively, or its integrity in the community that it serves.

Note that either of these minor situations could have resulted in serious consequences however if they did not cause injury or accidents they will be relegated to the minor incident category. A minor incident designation usually involves a low level supervisor speaking with the officer regarding your complaint, and getting the officers side of the story. Then a determination of founded or unfounded is made and the supervisor may tell the officer to watch his speed on residential streets. Speeding by police officers is one of the more popular issues reported by citizens. One reason is that officers drive 8 hours or more each day and the driving habits become more aggressive as they develop an overly confident driving profile.

Secondly officers from time, to time receive calls in which lights, and sirens would be a hindrance to effectively approaching a scene. Some crimes in progress require not alerting the suspects of police presence. An example is a burglary call. The officer at his discretion may exceed the speed limit in order to get to the scene as quickly as possible without turning on his lights or siren. The other side of the coin is that the state normally does not recognize an emergency vehicle with the authority to speed, run red lights or drive on the shoulders of the roadway unless both lights and sirens are engaged. So the officer you report for speeding may also receive a job well done for the same incident if he, or she gets to the burglary scene in time to stop the criminals. Many scenarios like this exist in the day to day life of a peace officer. In short, the low level supervisor may not be eager to reprimand an officer for speeding depending on the circumstance.

Formal Investigations are usually carried out by the Internal Affairs Division of the officers department. These are investigations deemed serious enough to require a more in depth process than a cursory conversation with a desk sergeant. An allegation of serious misconduct requires that the officer, or officers involved in the incident not contact any witnesses, or in any way participate in the investigation. A chain of command is strictly followed and the officer may need an attorney or union representative to be with him when he answers questions regarding the allegations. You as a reporting citizen should immediately report any contact from outside the normal avenues of the investigation. Meaning friends, or family of the accused officer. If you are followed, or you observe an officer watching or keeping you under surveillance get pictures if possible, and safe to do so. Remember to call the police 911 operators immediately. That way your voice and call are recorded, and retrievable.

Don't be discouraged if the proceedings take time, if there were other witnesses, or officers who may have been aware of what occurred they will need to be interviewed as well. If the police officers close ranks do not be surprised it is to be expected according to former St. Louis police officer Redditt Hudson, who recently wrote in an article that 15 percent of the policemen in any given department will do the right thing all the time. While 15 percent will be abusive, and make bad decisions all the time. He allows that 70 percent will follow whatever is the dominant position of the department leadership, and thereby fall into lock step with whomever is being supported by the police department leaders. This can mean that an astounding 85 percent of any given police departments officers may be a mortal threat to each, and every citizen they encounter on a day to day basis.

This situation highlights the need for effective reporting methods, and a well educated citizenry in regards as to how carry out their duties, and responsibilities when it comes to bettering our police departments around the country. For instance, what if you were to ride some form of public transportation, and the driver was operating the vehicle erratically, and speeding. You would quickly call them on it, and report him, or her with the full expectation that something would be done to curtail this driver before someone gets hurt. If we follow that form of logic, then we should expect that a police officer should be held to at least the same standard as a bus driver or garbage truck driver.

Your complaint may bring about criminal, or civil penalties and in some cases both can be levied. Cases such as these can take time, although they are quite different in that the standards of evidence are vastly different. In a criminal case the evidence has to be beyond a reasonable doubt, whereas in a civil case the burden of proof is established at 51 percent. Most attorneys will wait until an official decision is rendered by a criminal court before moving forward with a civil suit. Unless the evidence on its face is overwhelming. If an internal investigation is under way any indictment, or charges by the district attorney, may put internal investigations on hold once a civil case is filed. Often if the district attorney files criminal charges it results in the police officer involved being placed on leave or restricted duty until a verdict is reached. In the case of a not guilty verdict in a criminal trial a civil case can still be filed, and even won. If the verdict comes back guilty in a criminal trial the civil case tends to be much easier to win as again the threshold of evidence for guilt, or culpability is much higher in the criminal proceedings.

The District Attorney's office can be a formidable resource if you have a serious enough allegation. This office can independently initiate an investigation that is less likely to be tainted by any loyalties normally shared by officers. Note again that not every investigation results in an indictment. Often it is the result of the accusation and the subsequent investigation sitting in the officers personnel file that carries weight on correcting his behavior, or giving his supervisor enough cause to require the officer to report for remedial training.

Many departments have tracking systems in place to monitor for unusually high complaints on an officer, as compared to other officers who work in the same areas. This on its face seems like a good faith effort to identify officers who need to be relieved of duty, or given further training but if the commanding officers in the department want this particular type of officer then that is what they will protect.

Another point of contention is that officers don't hold each other accountable. The silence on one side of the thin blue line is deafening. In some instances, independent investigators can be assigned with the authority to carry investigations forward regardless of any investigations in the police department or their findings.

Think about what desired outcome will bring you satisfaction. Be reasonable in your assessments of how you may have been damaged, or inconvenienced. At some point you, or your representative may be asked questions regarding what you hope to achieve by going through the processes of reporting the officer, requesting that criminal charges be brought, or filing a civil suit. These are all concerns. Some people just want an apology, others desire punitive damages, while someone else just wants the system to work so that the abuse comes to an end. There are many possible scenarios but realistically your number one choice may not be achievable with your complaint alone. It may take two or three other complaints to solidify a reasonable outcome to a given problem.

Does this mean you should give up? By all means no, but keep in mind that your part in the process is important. If mediation becomes necessary try and have at least 3 to 4 outcomes that you can accept as closure. Mediation may be an attempt to settle out of court in the case of a civil suit, or if an internal investigation shows a high probability of wrong doing on the part of the officer. You may be approached regarding what you require in order to bring the matter to a conclusion. Get everything in writing and in some cases it may be wise to use the services of an attorney. If the investigation returns a finding of unfounded you may have the right to appeal the decision in certain instances. Questions like this should be asked when you are interviewed by the investigating officer. Make certain that you have the name and contact information for whomever your contact person is in the department may be as it relates to updates, and the final disposition of the complaint that you filed.

As explained previously a complaint has several effects first and foremost it sits in an officers jacket whether it is founded, unfounded, proven, or unproven. Secondly it becomes a red flag to anyone reviewing the officers file for promotion, upgrade in pay, merit increases, future disciplinary investigations, future criminal investigations, and in some cases contract renewal. Whether the officer receives a verbal reprimand, written reprimand, suspension without pay, demotion, or nothing at all the bottom line is that your complaint matters if you see it through, and are diligent, and informed about the process.

Third party complaints are harder to get traction unless the person who was injured, or wronged is a minor, or elderly, or incapacitated in some way which prevents them from complaining for themselves. This includes persons not in this country legally, the mentally, or physically challenged, or even individuals who may have warrants and are afraid to come forth for fear of being arrested in retaliation for complaining. Otherwise the allegation has to be of a very serious nature in order for the investigatory process to begin.

One the rare occasion that your encounter with law enforcement is with an off duty officer it is paramount that you try and get and remember the police officers name. Eventually the police from the jurisdiction that you are in will have to become involved. You can ask for the off duty officers name, and department. If this information is denied you at least you have the name of the officer on the street who is wearing a name tag and who's report will bear his, or her badge number. This is good fall back in case any attempt is made to protect the offending off duty officers identification and department information. You should file a complaint with the offending off duty officers agency, and make certain to contact city council members, and someone in the hierarchical structure of both departments.

Off duty officers are held to the same standards as uniformed officers, and are subject to the same powers of review as it relates to their conduct. Even in these situations with off duty law enforcement personnel it is important to remember that the street is not where the battle is won. You must put them in a place where their guns, tasers, and asp batons are useless and that is not the street.

Agencies are required to put forth a good faith effort to identify an officer if you do not have his name. If necessary you may have to challenge the excuse of not being able to identify an officer if the effort was not made in the spirit of the law, or in good faith. Seek department documentation of what steps were taken to find the officer in question. It may require that a suit against the department be filed so that the power of a subpoena is brought to bear against any resistance to your search.

Never complain anonymously unless the complaint bears the weight of the most serious of allegations it will be summarily dismissed. *I often think of my brother being pulled over every morning on his way to work by the same police officer who would hold him until he knew he had made him late his new job. This went on for over a week before the owner of the company made one call to the city council member over the area. And then it stopped forever in the case of my brother.* How many more motorist are harassed like this or worse? How many lost their jobs, or were possibly generationally affected by this abusive police officer? As a police officer nothing embarrassed me more than a relative or friend telling me how they were mistreated by one of my fellow sworn officers for absolutely no reason.

My god daughter was harassed in the same way by an officer in the same department I worked for his behavior was despicable and her young son witnessed the entire incident as this wolf in a uniform lied, humiliated her and then wrote her a citation. I told her fight the ticket but we both knew it was the sworn police officer's word against hers and the judge would, and did believe the lying officer over the citizen who was unjustly ticketed.

Without proper reporting by the citizens this kind of damage can go on for years. I have to wonder how long the officer in my brother's case had made it a practice to pull over black men and detain them until they were late. The final nail in the coffin is he was probably not alone in the practice and had bragged to his peers about what he was doing. And as I said before not one of them cared enough about their oath of office to uphold the law, and the constitution or to protect an innocent college student struggling to be successful.

The cowards probably laughed right along and did not say or do anything about it. To the police officer reading this if you have ever wondered why citizens across the country are turning against you all you have to do is look at your peers and be truthful, how many of them should be wearing a badge and why are they still in uniform?

It is long past time for us to save ourselves there is no help coming of any significance. So file your complaint, follow the guidelines, and encourage everyone you know to use the system we have in place for the good of the next victim.

Most officers build up to committing the most egregious offenses. Officers do not graduate from the police academy one day and molest, or beat a citizen the next week. The citizens willing to file, and pursue reports are the ones who save the next victims. And sometimes that may be the only saving grace we get to carry with us as we move forward from our abuser. At least we know that we played our part and that we played it well.

RISING VOICES

The following are tweets sent out by a police officer whose sudden honesty gives even more validity to an already thunderous cascade of accusations of mistreatment, from citizens concerning abuse on the part of police officers. What prompted his sudden desire to come forward with his observations is unknown. But the way it normally works is his career is over, and he will soon be fired. As you read the following tweets keep in mind that these are only some of the incidents of which he is aware, and are certainly not all inclusive of the department for which he works. In other words this is only the tip of the iceberg of wrongful convictions, physical assaults, violations of civil rights, and dehumanizing activities in which thousands of police officers participate, or know of and keep silent throughout this nation on a daily basis. And most disconcerting is the final tweet regarding the legal lynching of Black/ African American males through predatory policing on the part of officers who swore an oath to uphold the law, and the constitution.

Michael A. Wood Jr. @MichaelAWoodJr

A detective slapping a completely innocent female in the face for bumping into him, coming out of a corner chicken store.
10:01 AM - 24 Jun 2015

Punting a handcuffed, face down, suspect in the face, after a foot chase. My handcuffs, not my boot, or suspect
10:03 AM - 24 Jun 2015

Pissing and shitting inside suspects homes during raids, on their beds and clothes.
10:04 AM - 24 Jun 2015

Jacking up and illegally searching thousands of people with no legal justification
10:08 AM - 24 Jun 2015

Having other people write PC (probable cause) statements, who were never there because they could twist it into legality.

Swearing in court and PC (probable cause) docs that suspect dropped CDS (controlled deadly substances) during unbroken visual pursuit when neither was true.

Targeting 16-24 year old black males essentially because we arrest them more, perpetrating the circle of arresting them more.
10:11 AM - 24 Jun 2015

The availability of news stories, videos, and audio recordings of police officers, and citizen's interactions has begun to flood public websites, and media outlets with stories that in times past would not have made it past local networks. But the internet has taken incidents that often never would have been heard of into a classification known as "gone viral". Seeing a firsthand account of a 12 year old holding a toy pistol being shot to death in a public park has an effect worldwide.

Freethoughtproject.com
Pictured above a police officer who shot a 12 year old that was playing with toy gun in the park.

Video shows that the 12 year old child died 2 seconds after the police officer arrived on the scene. The officer stated that the boy refused to follow commands. The video looks like the police officer stepped out of the patrol car and shot him as soon as he got out of the patrol car. So the officers did not use a tactical approach to the scene. The officers did not use the public address system from a safe distance to instruct the child to drop his toy. The officer lied about the child's reaction to their commands. In short the police officer executed the child without ever giving him a chance to live. It is pretty much a no brainer to imagine that no one in this family will view police officers as trust worthy for the next 2 generations. Here is another example of an execution.
John Crawford

freethoughtproject.com

This picture shows an officer just before he kills a man holding a bb gun in Walmart in an open carry state. Video evidence showed that the man did not threaten anyone. And he was shot less than 1 second after police contact.

The man pictured above was holding bb gun in a Walmart where they are sold before he was executed less than 1 second into police contact. The incident happened in an open carry state and the Attorney General for the state advised that the man was not in violation of any law when he was shot.

Situations like these take on a life of their own and catch fire around the world in a matter of hours thanks to social media sharing on the internet. More than ever before an officer's actions can be scrutinized, judged, manipulated for profit, used to spur on feelings, and emotions of hate, and distrust, or feelings of thankfulness, and honor which I referenced under the "Professional" in the section on types of officers.

The previous images are compelling each in their own right. Each tells a story of a police officer who in a moment which required a judgment call made a decision that was not popular, and may have been illegal, and immoral at the very least.

Every legal decision is not the right decision, training guidelines are subject to the situation at hand.

The actions of good officers will be remembered for a season but the actions which have negative connotations will be reverberated much further, and with more passion than the good deeds.

Rough estimates say that about 50,000 people will be stopped by the police while operating a motor vehicle on a public road each day. Of that 50,000 it only takes one ill-advised decision on the part of the citizen, or officer to turn the routine into the disastrous. This decision can lead to a shooting, or a physically abusive arrest being made each helping to paint a negative image of the police across the nation.

I have broken down many videos and in far too many cases citizens try and take authority over an officer on the street. This is not an authority that any citizen has. Even in situations where an officer is wrong there is a line of demarcation that cannot be crossed without repercussions. These repercussions usually involves the officers use of force against a citizen such as striking, tasing, or shooting the citizen. An investigation may ensue during which the police officer is given paid leave until he is cleared of wrong doing because he had reasonable fear for his safety, or the safety of his peers.

A citizen is grievously injured, or mortally wounded, and the officer is not reprimanded because he has learned the lie most frequently quoted after a senseless shooting. ***Having feared for the safety of myself, and my fellow officers I deployed my duty weapon, and fired to stop the subject in order to prevent serious bodily harm, or death to anyone at the scene including myself.*** No one can read the officers mind as to what he was thinking at that moment we only have his word to rely on. The content of his heart cannot be discerned. But his character is known by his actions in the past. Other officers and supervisors in the department know if he makes racist jokes, laughs at rape victims, talks about how fast he will shoot people, or uses phrases like ***"It is better to be tried by 12 than carried by 6".***

Freethoughtproject.com

In the case of a citizen encounter turning physical there are no guidelines which state that an officer is required to fight a female, or a minor any differently than he would a 6'2" 210 lbs male, and nor should there be. Social sensibilities aside I have witnessed females crack policemen's heads wide open because the police officer was trying to be soft with a hardened criminal or an individual with malicious intent and nothing to lose at the moment. The previous image and the one below reflect however a completely different perspective as it relates to when an officer is within his rights to defend himself.

The woman being punched is 51 years old and is mentally unstable, the girl below is 15 years old and screaming for her mother, in both cases the police officers over reacted.

Freethoughtproject.com

This is done because under department policies, and state law the citizens refusal to cooperate with an officers command gives that officer certain rights in the threat escalation continuum to attack the citizen physically. One problem is that too many officers become comfortable with this image of being hardened, and cruel towards anyone who crosses, or does not comply with them. *Situations like these warn everyone that you don't mess with the police.* It also says to the average citizen that we don't care if you get hurt or abused as long as we are safe.

Adding insult to a perceived, and real injury becomes the death knell for mutual trust, mutual respect, and mutual considerations that police officers, and citizens require in order to have an orderly society. Citizens must be able to trust that officers are invested enough in the system to carry out their duties fairly, faithfully and fully. No shortcuts, no big I little you syndrome, and no turning the blinded eye to the abuses of other police officers. Just once I would like to see an officer arrest another officer on the spot for committing felony assault on an innocent citizen.

But now police officers shoot teenagers in the back and then high fived their dead bodies in open view of the public, and then lie about the incident.

Freethoughtproject.com

The constant reports of police officer abuses like these have opened the door for something much darker now. For the second time in my lifetime I hear voices rising which call for, and herald a new tone. A call to citizens to arm themselves, and fight back against abusive, and murderous police officers. This shrill cry carries with it calls for vigilantism against police officers, and an out and out defiance of police authority, as well as civil revolts against a system that seemingly bears no remorse, or concern for the needless atrocities committed under the cover of the badge.

The first time I heard this it was in rap albums under songs like "One in the chamber". It infuriated a lot of Americans, but *as the photos throughout this book have demonstrated the abuses that only one segment of society was complaining about in 1991 have overtaken the whole of our nation.* There are those who still support the police. I unashamedly am one such supporter, but I support good officers who do the job right, not the cowards, and killers. Cowards who won't speak up, and protect my children from the killers looking to orgasm through their guns every shift.

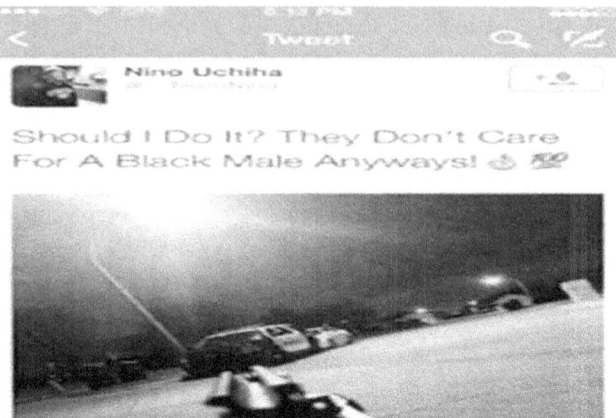

The photo above speaks for itself as an unwitting officer becomes a potential target as a black teen points a weapon at the patrol car and quires should he ambush the officer or not.

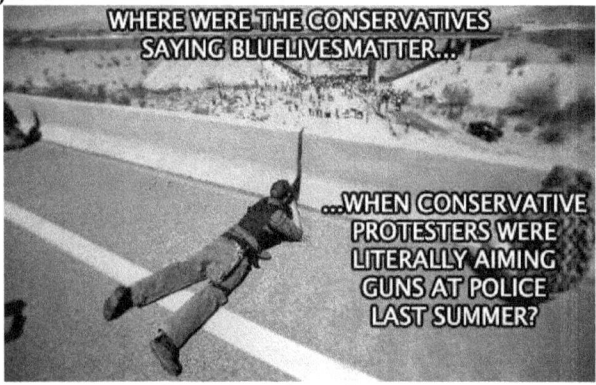

Freethoughtproject.com

Above we see citizens on opposite ends of the spectrum who have come to the same conclusion.

Rank and file police officers are not blind to the problems and some of them will speak out, but most will keep quiet for a regular pay check and health and dental benefits for their families.

I interviewed officers who divulged that command staff in certain divisions of the police department wanted the kind of aggressive officer who would develop a reputation on the street, a reputation of fear, and intimidation which goes ahead of them. One drug dealer I interviewed stated that "if you run from narcs in this town and they catch you, you gon catch a beat down." Another source told me that, "If narcs chase you, and you jump fences to get away, when they catch you, and handcuff you they don't walk you out of a gate and back to the street and to a patrol car. They pick you up, and throw you handcuffed over each fence you made them jump. Then they take you in for booking and if you are injured they say you did it going over the fence."

When you have a police captain, or higher who wants to protect this kind of police officer you can be certain that a lot of wood shampoos will be handed out. Most criminals charge this behavior to the game. It becomes what they expect from police. When the average citizen receives this kind of treatment they are completely unprepared for it. The citizen is in great fear of much worse happening to them or their families. The thought of a police officer calling my son a "nigger" and threatening to shoot him makes me angrier than words can express. Still I interview pastors, painters and school teachers who have endured this kind of treatment and worse at the hands of a wolf with a badge. The officers who don't do this but who's silence serves to protect the cowards in the department, and who are aware of his activities, and yet they cower in emasculation, and denial. Those officers whose voices would carry more weight, but are not moved enough as human beings to speak up. This lack of accountability has become unacceptable to American citizens. We now hear open calls for action grow louder daily. The call for action crosses cultural boundaries, socio economic backgrounds, and genders. It is strengthening daily as groups who once had little in common now have a common fear.

NYPD Stops by Race, 2004-2012

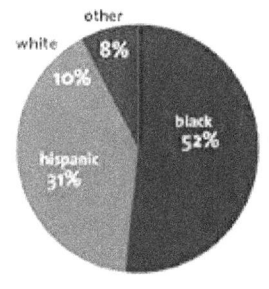

Source: Center for Constitutional Rights

According to the Center for Constitutional Rights
the chart above depicts the disparity that exists in New York City.

The statistic above reflects what goes on in America in disproportionate numbers in minority communities, and they leave little room for doubt as to why certain voices in the community are raised in such fervor against the police who have sworn an oath to serve and protect and defend the constitution.

Dr. Martin Luther King Jr. once said, "An injustice anywhere is a threat to justice everywhere". Due to social media, and the shift in media coverage toward acknowledging a more diverse populaces issues like the one in the graph above are being exposed, exploited, and politicized. To some extent the unaffected majority population is becoming more aware because the incidents of abuse have spread into its base as well.

There are those who would exploit this as purely a race issue but the real problem is a power shift toward governmental entities and away from the people. Americans have been described as pacified babies who are nourished on shallow political pabulum, while constructs are being put into place to engineer the demise of our country. And chief most to this insidious construct is having in place a disconnect between the people, and the state. Thus, a police state begins to emerge little by little so as not arouse those who feel secure in their social, political, and economic places. So, comfortable that in fact they feel no need to awake to the cries of injustice from another citizen because for now the bell does not toll for them.

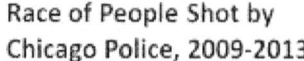

Race of People Shot by
Chicago Police, 2009-2013

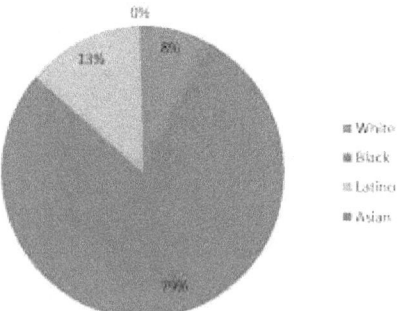

The graph above demonstrates the prior argument. How is it possible for the remaining 21 percent of Chicago's populace to not see a vast disparity.

Another criminal I interviewed had his nose, and jaw broken. He said that he had received the beating at the hands of police officers. As he told the story he further offered that he had knocked the two officers' unconscious prior to them assaulting him. He went on to say that he knew they were going to handcuff, and beat him so he got his licks in first, and then sat on the couch and waited on them to come too. He advised he had been smoking drugs, and did not care about going to jail because the beating he was going to take was just part of the way things worked. These are words from a known criminal. Note his aggression toward the officers was the only recourse he felt he had because even if he went peacefully he knew the officers would still rough him up. He had done time before, and due to his surroundings and training he was more than a match for most officers on the police force in that city.

This undercurrent of emotions, and feelings has been coming to the surface more, and more frequently in our country. These toxic explosions of anger, and malice have resulted in several ambush attacks against police officers across our nation. Some of these attacks have yet to be solved. One startling statement being expressed was "he didn't do nothin' wrong, he just shot a cop." Unfortunately, the prevailing mentality is shifting whereas once in this country shooting a policeman was the absolute last thing anyone wanted to do. *It has now become a threat that has created a hair trigger environment on the streets for police as well as citizens.*

The new open carry movement that is growing in popularity has served to increase the animosity as white open care advocates are interviewed briefly and go on their way while black open carry advocates are more likely to be ordered to the ground and taken in for questioning, or shot without provocation. This disparity in treatment reflects poorly on race relations between blacks, and whites in this country. In one protest federal officers had sniper rifles pointed at them during a land rights protest while black men have been shot to death for carrying a bb gun in an open carry state and to add insult to the death they were shot in the back.

Freethoughtproject.com

Pictured above is the crime scene where 2 Ferguson Missouri officers were ambushed in the midst of the upheaval regarding the shooting of Michael Brown.

Scenes like the one above are being played out across the country to the extent that congress has passed new laws which require the sharing of credible information across departmental lines when the lives of officers are being threatened. This safety measure on behalf of police officers comes at a time when as pictured below citizens on differing sides of the color line are taking aim at law enforcement quite literally.

Freethoughtproject.com

The photo above is the scene of a violent ambush on two police officers and a standoff with police by citizens who regarded violence as the most viable option left to them. The vitriol to carry out such brutality seems to emanate from communities across the nation. Which heretofore have appeared on opposite sides of the debate when it comes to law enforcement and its policies.

FBI statistics note that violent attacks and ambushes against police officers has risen over 50 percent in the past 2 years. Many of these attacks are ambush style attacks, which speaks to premeditation. What I believe is these are the voices of anger which rise up be heard when citizens feel that traditional avenues of reporting and investigations are bastardized into vehicles intended to cover for murderous savages who crept through the doors of the police department, and who are protected by cowards who would not want their families treated in the same manner that they know the curs are treating everyday citizens.

When there is no room for discourse...violence
becomes the megaphone of the oppressed

The evidence is undeniable social media is rife with calls for community violence against law enforcement officers. Voices which encourage extra judicial retribution on the part of citizens against abusive law enforcement officers are being entertained. These calls harken back to the days when rappers were encouraging violence against what they said were "dirty cops".

Freethoughtproject.com
Scenes like this are now being encouraged. This is what we must avoid.

There are problems, and unanswered questions with this myopic although seemingly reasoned view as it relates to the law of self-preservation. If retaliatory actions are taken against police officers, which ones are they taken against? All police officers are not abusive. As alluded to earlier in the article written by Reddit Hudson 15 % of the officers in the department will do the right thing all the time.

I certainly would not be in favor of harming them. 15% will choose to do the wrong thing i.e.... shoot you and lie about the circumstances, pull you over for being a minority, accuse you of resisting as an excuse to hit you, tase you, or strike you after you are handcuffed, tease you and harass you as they take you to jail and tow your vehicle, or add 10 extra miles to your speeding ticket because they can get away with it.

Officer Hudson's assertions seem to be backed up by Officer Michael Wood Jr. as he tweeted the unfair police practices of the Baltimore police department.

I find it interesting that more officers around the country are not coming out to try and right some of the wrongs committed by their brethren in blue. Certainly the life time tag of convicted felon will have generational effects on the men, and families who have suffered under the boots of these thugs.

Officer Wood Jr. clearly states that he has seen what we all know happens every day. Innocent people are set up by police officers.

Google Lenell Geter and read his story. It would seem more appropriate to go after the law breakers in uniform than to constantly let their violations be swept under the rug. Again, I am waiting to see an officer arrest one of his cohorts after an abusive outburst and hand cuff him, take his weapon and put him in the back seat as he would any other law breaker.

But I do not expect it due to the level of cowardice, and the desire for self preservation as well as a lack of desire to commit career suicide.

A recent quote from a news contributor stated that not all Germans were aggressive bloodthirsty killers, the aggression was not the desire of the majority but it was their silence that made them irrelevant, the same can be said of Islam if most Muslims are peaceful but silent about the atrocities committed by the few extremists in their number and lastly Christians are to be held to the same standard.

It can be said then that they too are irrelevant. So, it is with the silent 70% of police officers. Their silence has made them irrelevant.

These miscreants need to be separated from their badges as soon as possible. By this I mean through the reporting process, and by the department itself raising the standards of professional conduct, and not accepting anything less ever again.

The conundrum is what to do with the other 70 percent of police officers who go along with whatever standard of conduct they have communicated to them by the higher ups. I feel that the silent majority are as guilty as the aggressive embarrassments who hide behind a shield.

freethoughtproject

If one of the other officers on scene had gotten to this man before he lost control he might still be employed today and this young girl would not have been abused

All officers have a responsibility to their oath of office, and to the public they swore to protect. I don't know if there is room for the 70 percent of silent cowards who will stand by and let another officer wrongfully kill, or beat my sons head in just for the sake of a paycheck and a badge. All policemen are not the same, just as all citizens are not the same. I had a corporal tell me that he witnessed a police officer about to hit a teenage boy with his night stick when the boy's father spoke from the crowd and said, "if you hit him I will kill you". He then told his son to go with the officer and not to resist. The officer took the boy in without any further incident. This took place in a small Georgia town. The difference in the officer's treatment of the boy was the very real threat that the father meant what he said, and would follow through with it on the spot. The officer recognized a power, or a force on the boys' side that he did not want to come to bear against him despite his legal authority.

The perception of being powerless victims in certain communities is where the cry of helplessness makes money for the flatulent mouth pieces who attempt to pass for leaders. This tends to bleed into the way that residents of that community are treated by police officers who patrol their neighborhoods. Statistics bear this out. The more recent voices that are given the platform call for a much more radical agenda than to tout victimhood. One which speaks to the same frustrations demonstrated in other areas of the world where the people truly have no voice. Thus the only language left to them is violence, and ultimately rebellion. Evidence is mounting of this same disruptive mentality creeping into the communities in which officers are portrayed as abusive, and dangerous. As is evident by the groups of individuals who have begun forming in efforts to expose wrong doing by filming police officers.

Groups like thefreedomthoughtproject.com, Cop Watch, Copblock.org, Filming Cops, Countercurrentnews.com, Police Brutality Corruption in America, and Americans Against Police Brutality.

Less than a year ago I was approached by an individual who advised the invitation to join a group that he was affiliated with would only be extended one time, and if it was turned down it would not be repeated ever. It was a little unnerving to hear what they wanted to do. I don't do groups, too many leaks. But their intent was to protect their families, and take retribution on anyone who wrongfully attacked any member of the group. It sounded like a gang to me but he was referring to law enforcement. He was quite honest in his assertion that some people would not be invited because they tend to attract abuse by acting in such a manner as to endanger themselves, and there by exacerbate an already bad situation. That in and of itself is bad enough but the groups feelings was that there are instances where law abiding citizens with no intent of wrong doing are singled out, and abused, or killed. He bought up the case of John Crawford III where it looked to be nothing more than an execution. He also mentioned Jason Mahe who was shot 7 times in the back after telling the officers that he had a toy gun in his pocket, and when asked to show it he did so but dropped it to the ground before being shot. I was most shocked at the race of the person with the invite. He was not black as I would have expected. In any case I am not a member, but I have the same concerns for my sons, and daughter as that man has for his. I have taught my sons to comply immediately with any law enforcement officer who has a constitutionally sound request. I have also taught them that the street is not where you fight an officer unless that officer turns it into a life, and death struggle. I further told them that most of the cowards who would do you harm are going to make certain that they have the upper hand before making a move so be alert, use the tools that I have given you, and know that your main agenda is to survive the moment. Knowing full well that your father has your back if you are in the right.

CONSTITUTIONAL AMENDMENTS

1st Amendment: Congress shall make no law respecting an establishment of religion, or prohibiting the free exercise thereof; or abridging the freedom of speech, or of the press, or the right of the people peaceably to assemble, and to petition the Government for a redress of grievances.

Guarantees the right to the freedoms of speech, press, and religion. Protects the right to petition the government as well as the freedom to assemble.

This right allows to you to say within reason whatever you want. Beware that profanity can get you a citation for disorderly conduct in some states. In Seattle Washington the Supreme Court recently ruled that a police officer cannot be offended, and arrest a citizen for obstruction when the citizen's only action is to criticize the officer's job performance no matter what words are used even if it is explicit profanity. This may not be the case in every state.

http://www.seattletimes.com/seattle-news/crime/court-first-amendment-protects-profanity-against-police/
http://www.aele.org/law/2011all10/2011-10MLJ101.pdf

2nd Amendment: A well regulated Militia, being necessary to the security of a free State, the right of the people to keep and bear Arms, shall not be infringed.

Guarantees the people's right to own, and bear arms for their defense. States laws have usurped, and infringed some of the original intent but on face value it was the citizens responsibility to make sure the State continued to have freedom, and that required arms equal to the task, or in other words on par with military weapons. The recent attention that open carry, and concealed carry hand gun permits speak to the perceived need for extra security that Americans feel is missing in their day to day lives.

4th Amendment: The right of the people to be secure in their persons, houses, papers, and effects, against unreasonable searches and seizures, shall not be violated, and no Warrants shall issue, but upon probable cause, supported by Oath or affirmation, and particularly describing the place to be searched, and the persons or things to be seized.

Citizens cannot be forced to subject themselves to seizure, and search without a search warrant, and probable cause. The laws and practices which allow for the Terry Stop or Stop and Frisk get very close to the edge here. The Terry Stop was meant to protect the safety of officers who had suspicion, but not probable cause as they encountered persons who could be nefarious but who had not risen to the level of probable cause. Be careful in these incidents to let the officer know where the boundary line is. A piece of paper in your pocket is not a weapon and does not threaten his safety. He may think it is drugs but unless he has some other mitigating evidence the citizen has the right to say, "I do not give you permission to search inside my pockets". In December, 2014 the Supreme Court ruled that an officer's violation of the 4th amendment did not make void the fruit of a search during a traffic stop which was not legal, and that said evidence could be used to prosecute said individual. In short if an officer does not know the law his violation of your rights is waived. It will be interesting to see if the Supreme Court revisits this as it gives law enforcement carte blanche to claim ignorance of the law as a precursor to violating the 4th amendment at will. This excuse will soon fall into the pile with "you fit the description" "I felt my life was in danger" and others that are over used lies.

http://thefreethoughtproject.com/supreme-court-rules-citizens-protection-violations-cops-ignorant-law/

Many constitutional experts are strongly opposed to this view that "ignorance of the law on the part of the one who is supposed to be enforcing the law, or constitution is an excuse for violations of such and bear no penalty under the law. These overreaches may play out differently in the civil courts if one can prove damages due to the lack of training provided by the department. This particular ruling is believed to violate the 4th amendment right against unreasonable searches and seizures by the government. It also opened the door of intent on the part of the law enforcement officer. What was the officer original intent? Was there a clear intent to violate the law or the constitution? How far is not considered too far, or how far can the search go before it is considered grossly over reaching and abusive. This may move from vehicle traffic stops to other property or home searches. And to add insult to injury it is near impossible to make a law enforcement entity pay for the damage caused by a search. That is one reason I never commit to searches of any kind. Get a warrant.

5th Amendment: No person shall be held to answer for a capital, or otherwise infamous crime, unless on a presentment or indictment of a Grand Jury,

except in cases arising in the land or naval forces, or in the Militia, when in actual service in time of War or public danger; nor shall any person be subject for the same offence to be twice put in jeopardy of life or limb; nor shall be compelled in any criminal case to be a witness against himself; nor be deprived of life, liberty, or property, without due process of law; nor shall private property be taken for public use without just compensation.

Prohibits abuse of governmental authority in legal procedures. Establishes rules for indictment by eminent domain and grand jury. Guarantees the due process rights. Protects citizens from self-incrimination and double jeopardy.

The rights of the common citizen to refuse to talk to law enforcement is frequently bullied away from the citizen under threat of arrest. One video I watched made my blood boil as the officer threaten the take the couples baby away because he wanted to run the passenger for wants and warrants on a traffic stop and the passenger told him his business was with the driver on what was a very weak if not fabricated traffic stop altogether. The police officer if operating within the bounds of information he had that was credible could have explained. But his ego would not let him conduct himself as a professional, so another citizen was abused, and threatened.

6th Amendment: In all criminal prosecutions, the accused shall enjoy the right to a speedy and public trial, by an impartial jury of the state, and district wherein the crime shall have been committed, which district shall have been previously ascertained by law, and to be informed of the nature and cause of the accusation; to be confronted with the witnesses against him; to have compulsory process for obtaining witnesses in his favor, and to have the assistance of counsel for his defense.

 Guarantees the citizen a fair, and speedy trial, and the right to know the accusation or accusations against them, as well as the identity of the accuser, and the right to counsel, and witnesses.

The question every citizen should ask an officer at first contact is am I being detained, what laws am I suspected of breaking or crime am I suspected of having committed, am I free to leave. If you are being detained the officer will say so. At that point ask what suspicion or evidence he has that a crime is being committed has been committed or is about to be committed. He may not like it and he may even rebuke you for asking but you will need this interaction in case you have to file a complaint latter. Don't agitate the officer but be firm and let him know that you need answers since your freedom is apparently at risk.

8th Amendment: Forbids exorbitant bails and fines and punishment that is unusual or cruel.

Excessive bail shall not be required, nor excessive fines imposed, nor cruel and unusual punishments inflicted. I am waiting to see if this is challenged in court where a small town I know of with less than 15,000 residents can charge 1000 dollars for a nonhazardous traffic violation. It has yet to be appealed to a higher court.

SCENARIOS

The following are scenarios in which you may find yourself in as it relates to interactions with law enforcement. They are not all inclusive. Hopefully they can serve as a guide to help you better communicate with police officers, and survive the encounter.

Some ground rules for communicating with police officers. These guidelines lay the ground work for your successful interactions with law enforcement. They will serve as the foundation for effective recourse should you need to pursue any grievances.

Read the officers name tag, try and remember the badge number as well

Do not speak in a disrespectful manner, or threaten the officer.

Do not reach anywhere in the vehicle without telling the officer where you are reaching, even if he or she has requested the information.

Do not use street jargon, or slang. It can lead to inaccurate assumptions about who you are, or what you are doing and subsequently how you will be treated.

Do not try and over talk the officer, or out talk the officer.

Remember you don't have to say anything.

Remember you have recourses available to correct whatever the officer is attempting to do on the street. His authority and power are useless when he is standing before a review board, or internal affairs.

He or she may inconvenience you for a few moments but your complaint becomes a permanent part of his or her personnel file throughout their career. Every promotion consideration, every consideration for merit increase, even in the offering of another contract for employment your complaint and that of other citizens will reflect the kind of officers they are.

Try to avoid at all costs getting into a fight with a policeman on the street. Even if they say they will take off their badge and gun with no strings attached. **DO NOT DO IT UNLESS YOU KNOW FOR CERTAIN THAT YOUR LIFE IS IN**

EMINANT DANGER. No police officer has a right to play judge, jury and executioner with the lives of citizens on the street.

SCENERIO # 1. You are pulled over by a police officer who approaches your vehicle and asks for your driver's license, and proof of insurance. The officer neglects to mention why he pulled you over which is one of the first things he is supposed to do. What do you say.

Officer Smith my insurance card is in my glove box I need to get it out. While I'm getting it can you tell me why I'm being detained.

This response is cooperative and courteous and it holds him legally accountable to tell you why he stopped you. If his response is snide or discourteous such as I will get to that I don't need you telling me how to run my traffic stop. (You should expect this because most officers are afraid of looking like they are not in control.)

Officer Smith I would not insult you by pretending to know your job but I do know my rights, and the question was why was I stopped.

Be courteous but firm. The officer has a legal responsibility that he needs to perform, and letting you know why he stopped you is one of the primary responsibilities. Once you know why you were pulled over you can make up your mind how you will proceed. The officer may ask where you are going, or where you are coming from. If he does it is totally up to you if you want to answer. You can choose to exercise your 5th amendment right and say nothing, or you can answer some questions but not others. Officers may act frustrated with your refusal but it is part of the job of being a police officer. The lower caliber officers will try and find a way to inconvenience you, search you, or even say that you fit the description of someone they are looking for as means of putting the screws to you. Be as polite as possible, and understand that you will soon be placing a permanent mark in his personnel file by which he can remember you.

You fit the description is the biggest lie policemen tell.

Also note that generally the public is not privy to the information an officer has access to. And the excuse "you fit the description of someone we are looking for is over used, and unfairly applied by police officers who would rather lie than let you go, but sometimes a person can, and does fit the description of another person that may be wanted. This would be a great time to ask for a supervisor, and verify the officer's claims. If the supervisor substantiates the officer's claims get both names, and badge numbers and pursue the matter with an official complaint, or if a report is filed you can request a copy through the freedom of information act.

I know of one young man who was made to stand outside his car in the dead of winter, and wait while a witness was driven across town in the back of a police car to look at him. He in no way "fit the description of the robber other than he had on a white hoodie. *The young man being identified was 5'7" and weighed about 250 lbs. and the suspect described by the witness was over 6' tall and weighed about 180 lbs. Even the witness was perturbed at having their time wasted for such an obvious miscue.* The actual description of the true assailant only came out because other circumstances required a police report be written and the officer had to try and establish probable cause for pulling into Jack in the Box and taking three men out of a vehicle who were eating no moving violations, no expired registrations, and no calls for assistance. When the victim said that the young man in the white hoodie was not the robber the officer then tried to say the three men in the car had changed clothes and that another young man in the car was the suspect. The witness advised the officer that the second man was too short and skinny to be the robber. The third subject in the car was white and was totally out of the color spectrum of the robber.

This whole scenario points to the fact that police have information which we do not and they sometimes use it to harass, and abuse citizens at their discretion. That is how you go from a lone African American robber to two black men and a white man in a car on the opposite side of town being suspects for eating at Jack in the Box *because "you fit the description".*

SCENERIO # 2. An officer pulls over the car you are riding in. He tells the driver that they are being pulled over for a traffic violation but he wants to see identification from everyone in the car. You are one of the passengers.

Officer Smith, if this is a traffic stop then your business is with the driver. Am I suspected of committing a crime? Are you detaining me as a suspect? Am I free to leave? And if I can't leave what crime am I suspected of committing?

Expect an angry response due the egotistical nature of most policemen who as I said earlier they believe they "are the law, not enforcers of the law so whatever they say, or want becomes the law at that moment." The officer may then become verbally abuse by using profanity, and demand your identification as a way of intimidating you, or the officer may threaten to arrest you for failing to identify yourself to an officer. He may even refuse to tell you why he wants your identification in this totally unrelated traffic stop. He actually wants it so he can run you for warrants. This is a way lazy police officers show productivity on his shift. He is hoping to get a positive hit on warrants from anyone in the car. Some officers look for car loads of people to pull over just for this purpose. If the officer says that you are being detained you must turn over your identification even if you have not committed a crime.

Officers have the right to initiate physical contact with you by striking you, or using mace, or a baton against you for refusing to comply with their request and if you try and push their hands way or put your hands on them in any manner you can be charged with assault on a peace officer. When the officer writes his report he will make whatever slight contact you made into an aggressive attack against his person even if he has to lie to do it. Once a police officer attempts to arrest you and you offer any resistance you now have resisting arrest charges to contend with as well. In short give them the ID but again let it be known that you do so under protest of your constitutional rights being violated. This action on your part will not bode well for the officer if you have to file a complaint on him later. The officers getting his way only seem like victories on the street but the street is not where you the citizen has the most power. The pen is mightier than the sword in the right environment.

Example: *Officer I am surrendering my identification under protest because you are violating my constitutional rights and placing me under threat of even more illegally motivated actions.*

This verbal protest will come in handy later when you file a complaint on the officer. Make note of any remarks the officer makes regarding your protest so that you can quote him or her in your complaint. In 99% of the cases they will have a snide comment to your complaint which will only serve as more egg on their faces when they have to answer for it.

One officer told me that certain officers in his department would openly joke that all they had to do was follow a young black man in a car until he turned without using a signal, did not signal within the legal distance before turning, changed lanes without signaling, or if they could not see his inspection sticker as they passed any excuse or lie would do. And the fruit of all this was a chance to run him for warrants, or to write him a citation as way of showing productivity on their shift. They left the police department parking lot looking for young black males as their first priority. Should you find yourself in this position remember the officers name, and badge number for your complaint of (pick one below).

Abuse of Power   Official Misconduct
Civil Rights Violations   Official Oppression
Illegal Search and Seizure   Discrimination
Harassment
Unlawful Detention
Violation of Department Rules
Intimidation and Coercion

You still need to comply with the officer but you should verbally state that you are following his orders under protest, and that your rights are being violated. Again know that the street is not the place to have a physical confrontation with a police officer even if it's a rights issue. His personnel file, and internal affairs are where he is most vulnerable. I recommend contacting a city council member, or an investigative reporter who can make freedom of information act requests about the officer and see if the officer has a history of civil rights violations. You can make the same request as a citizen but there may be attempts to delay your request, or charge you an absurd amount for copies.

SCENERIO # 3. An officer approaches your vehicle after stopping you for speeding and uses profanity or racial slur toward you when asking for your license. Example...*Alright give me your license and insurance asshole. And where in the hell do you think you're going in such a hurry.*

Officer Smith I don't know what kind of day you're having but I'm not a profanity user and I hope we can move forward without it. Here is my license, I need to go into the glove box to get my insurance information is that alright with you?

You should receive compliance with your request without any further unnecessary abuses. If you are asked why just let them know that you prefer not to communicate in that manner. If the officer continues ask for a supervisor, and be sure to file a complaint. This use of abusive language is just the beginning of devaluing a person as a human being and denying them the respect they deserve and thereby their rights, and liberty.

Survive Police Contact

Few officers graduate from the Police Academy and jump right into abusing citizens they gradually move into that mode of thinking and operating one citizen contact after another until it becomes second nature to take advantage of citizens.

What happens when an officer starts a contact with you in a verbally abusive manner is that it can quickly degrade into physical abuse. Wolves circle their prey they don't just charge straight in. Likewise abusive officers tend to circle their victims. They are evaluating your responses to their questions, they are looking at your mannerisms.

How are you dressed, are you tatted from wrist to neck and beyond, are you showing some gang affiliation, are you avoiding eye contact, or being ambiguous with your answers to their questions. Their evaluation of you can make a world of difference in how far the officer believes he can go.

Your best weapon is what we call the queens English, a polite non-threatening response to any questions also helps. Do not allow yourself to become emotional and began shouting at the officer it only serves to further irritate, and provoke him. There is a place, and time to address his rude behavior, and abusive tactics but it is not on the street.

Know your current city council members name and office phone number written on something in your wallet. When you call them explain what happened and ask for their support in getting this reviewed by the appropriate people in city, or county government. I programmed a very aggressive local investigative journalist's phone number into my phone for just such an occasion.

In order to redirect his behavior you may choose to call for a supervisor and advise the officer that you will be taking this up with internal affairs as soon as possible. This can be a double-edged sword in that if he, or she are the worst of the worse they may choose to find reason to arrest, or attempt to hurt you. If the officer has had issues with Internal Affairs before they may back off from being physical. You have to judge the moment, and who you are dealing with. A younger officer will usually back off, but an old wolf has been there before and may choose to ratchet up his, or her aggression for the perceived threat.

SCENERIO #4. During a traffic stop, or a stop and frisk an officer begins to assault you.

Have you been compliant?

Have you provoked his anger?
Have you challenged him physically?
How many officers are there and did he call for back up?
Is the officer grabbing you and shoving you against a wall, or to the ground?
Is he punching you?
What is he saying….I will kick your ass, I will kill you, get on the ground, I will fuck you up, stop resisting?
Is he reaching for his gun while grabbing you with one hand?
Is he reaching for a taser while grabbing you with one hand?
Is he holding handcuffs in one hand while grabbing you?
Is he reaching for his lapel mic on his radio, or has he already called for backup before becoming physical.
Has he run you down after you tried to escape?

All these are determining factors in your next move, and your life may depend on it. It is a hectic situation and you must act quickly and move without hesitation. You need to know is this a survival situation or can it be de-escalated.
Should you choose de-escalation and you have practiced what I said previously then you know the officers name. Use it. Use it loudly and try and call him back from the frenzied state of mind that he has allowed to possess him.

Officer Smith what do you need me to do? Officer Smith what do you need me to do?

Officer Smith I'm trying to comply what do you need me to do.
If there are other officers there ask; *Can someone get him under control.*

This is done to bring liability for the officer's actions onto the other officers at the scene when you asked for help. If they do not help and you are genuinely being abused they become co-defendants in any criminal, civil, or disciplinary cases that may come forth.

He has never heard those words before, he has heard "get off me pig" "let me go" "stop" and a hundred other quotes that mean nothing to him in the moment. But a request for instructions coupled with his name will make him think. You have to reach his cognitive self. He is in attack mode right now, and his report will be filled with lies of how you made him feel threatened, or tried to fight him, maybe even how you tried to reach for his weapon.

He won't remember anything for sure, not even how many times he hit or kicked you in the face. You need that moment for him to come to a sense of composure, and respond verbally to your questions. It may be enough to cause him to stop the physical attack.

If he gives instructions comply immediately, and do not resist, or try and get an explanation out of him as to his actions. You already know that you will file a complaint. Be sure to take pictures of your injuries ASAP. You will probably be taken to jail but the processing will require you be photographed facially at least. If you can convince him to take you to a hospital for treatment. Neck, and chest pain will guarantee you a ride there.

Ask the nurse, or doctor to please photograph your injuries and list a family member who can have full access to your medical records. The police are not obligated to call your family right away and probably will not. Ask for a chaplain explain the situation and ask them to call your family ASAP.

If you have a family attorney ask that they be called as well. Don't wait till you are released to ask for an internal affairs officer to make your complaint. You want them to get to you immediately. Offer to take a polygraph, and quote the officer verbatim if he was saying something inappropriate.

Quote the officers who were standing by if they were there, and did not render assistance. If one tried to dissuade the attack offer that information as well. Usually there is not much sympathy on the part of the other officers. They are afraid of losing face with their piers the wolves, and the curses in uniform

If you find that the officer is not responding to your calling out his name, and trying to comply with getting on the ground and not resisting the police officer is either trying to render you unconscious, hospitalize you or kill you. Pretending to be unconscious may bring a halt to the beating but in doing so it can leave you completely defenseless to the blows and kicks at your head, face, and neck.

One of the largest men I have ever personally known told me of being taken to a field in the far reaches of the city he lived in. During his arrest he had physically intimidated the officers before complying and letting them handcuff him. He told me that he would never try and hurt a cop again. He told me how the officers called out for others to meet them at a predetermined location on the north side of the city he lived in and that while keeping him handcuffed they and almost beat him to death. He remembered about 6 squad cars each with 2 men in them arriving and then being removed from the patrol car, and attacked. He said he was left in the field possibly to die he was not sure, he said that he thought he would die before he found the edge of the road on his hands and knees since his eyes were beaten shut. He did not tell the doctors at the hospital who had done this to him.

When the police were called he just said that he got into it with some "dudes that I did not know them and that's all I remember". I could still see the fear in his eyes as he recalled his experience. He knew then that the police would kill him, and that he was lucky to survive that night so he said that he would never try and hurt or intimidate a policeman again ever.

I see in his story several troubling signs, the officers involved were already aware of where to meet to carry out the deed thus demonstrating premeditation. The already agreed upon activity requiring no discussion says that it was not the first time this group of men had done this. All that was required was to get a call via radio undoubtedly in code to meet there.

This was how wolves in uniform hunt in packs choosing to act as if they were judge, jury, and executioners instead of law enforcement officers. Without doubt if anyone of them were to be repaid in kind for their actions the whole of the law enforcement community would be up in arms. Fund raisers for the families, and vows to catch whoever did this to a good cop.

If the man who told me this story had died not one eye would have been batted or any help given his family by the back the blue crowd.

No one can make your decision for your and there will be consequences for you no matter what decision you make. So your choice becomes how do you survive?

Do you trust that this out of control man will stop short of killing you, or maiming you permanently, or do you try and fight back.

In Texas, there are statutes written into law which justify the use of force against a law enforcement officer if they are illegally searching, or arresting you, or if they are using excessive force to effect a search, or arrest. The moment you began physically resisting a police officer it is a life, and death struggle. There is no middle ground for compromise you are all in. One police officer told me that every call he goes on is a deadly force situation because he brings a gun with him to the scene. From the most minor traffic violations, to the bloodiest fights of the day everything he does is a deadly force situation because of his presence.

Texas Penal Code Chapter 9, Subchapter C, Section 9.31, Subsection C:
(c) The use of force to resist an arrest or search is justified: (1) if, before the actor offers any resistance, the peace officer (or person acting at his direction) uses or attempts to use greater force than necessary to make the arrest or search; and (2) when and to the degree the actor reasonably believes the force is immediately necessary to protect himself against the peace officer's (or other person's) use or attempted use of greater force than necessary.

Below is a perfect example of a citizen's right to resist but the cowards chose a 12 year old girl for their next victim

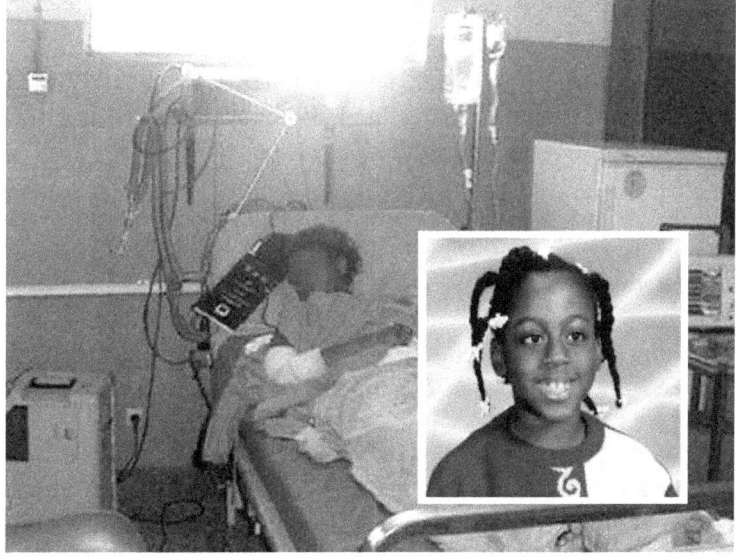

The picture you see is a 12 year old girl taken from her front yard and beaten by police officers who accused her of being a prostitute. Her name is Dymond. She was admitted at an area hospital. The plainclothes officers were in an unmarked van, and allegedly never identified themselves, to the child. When her father ran out of the house he too was assaulted. The original call was for 3 white females who were soliciting in the area. The examining physician found that the girl had injuries from multiple blows to the head, face, neck, lower back, left shoulder, and left hip/waist area. She suffered a contusion to the back of the head (where she was struck with a flashlight). There were abrasions on her arm and wrist. The 12 year old girls throat was swollen; she had difficulty swallowing, nausea and vomiting, and hoarseness of voice due to being struck in the throat. She had black eyes, scalp lacerations, tenderness of the vertebrae. She was experiencing double vision and loss of hearing. Dymond's ear drum and nose were also injured (blood in ear, bruised nasal septum, and nose bleed).

Ask any police officer in the country if three men grabbing their 12 year old daughter from their front yard with her screaming daddy help me would live longer than 10 seconds. To the last man they each would say all of three kidnappers die right there even if it cost them their lives as well. But you as a citizen are expected to offer no resistance, and let three unidentified men claiming to be police officers just take you child away in an unmarked van while they beat her senseless right in front of you.

Texas Penal Code Chapter 9, Subchapter C, Section 9.31, Subsection C: Says that these Galveston police officers can and should be resisted to whatever level necessary to stop them from effecting an unlawful, and abusive arrest. The paper thin lie the officers gave was laughable.

After the little girl was released from the hospital the maggots with badges showed up and arrested her from her classroom at school and charged her with resisting arrest on the day they beat her into a hospital.

This was nothing short of intimidation of a witness and the federal authorities should have been notified. The families' attorney says that the 12 year old girl and her father had a right to resist because of the excessive force that was being used on the child, and the unlawfulness of the arrest.

This is the situation where you fight the wolves to the bitter end. That being said we will enter into the evaluation of skill section of this chapter.

Survive Police Contact

The following information comes very hard for me to divulge due to the nature of the consequences. If you are thrust into a deadly force situation and you don't know if you will live, or die. You could at best be severely hurt, or maimed, or if you truly believe that the possibility of death is real. Ask yourself are ready to die. *Yes die.* If not what choices do you have for survival. I lost a friend who was choked to death by an officer who knew the young man was unresponsive but held his choke hold like a death clutch anyway just to make sure the young man died. He never faced any charges, or discipline.

This erupted over a dispute with a prostitute regarding 10 dollars for sex and it ended with a young man being killed by a wolf wearing a badge. Should you find yourself in this position and you choose to fight in a one on one against a police officer here is what to expect: *you will be hurt, you may go to jail for a long time, you may be killed.* This is why I advocate being polite, and submitting so that you can fight where he cannot shoot you, and claim you were lunging for his weapon.

Your skills as a fighter are honed over time. They do not suddenly come upon you because you are desperate. Use the following barometer to measure your chances for survival. *And always remember that in most cases your most powerful survival tool is your compliance with the officer's commands. Even if he is out of line. A bruised ego will heal a bullet in the head will not.* Be smart enough to pick the place to fight and don't let it be the street.

1. How strong are you?
2. How much can you squat or bench press?
3. How hard are your knuckles?
4. How do you react to pain?
5. Are your adept at fighting? (not the Queensbury rules)
6. When was your last fight?
7. Have you ever fought to the death before?
8. How quick are your hands?
9. Is there anything you would hesitate to do to survive?
10. Can you take a hard punch? (Not a jab)
11. Are you willing to do serious jail time?
12. Can your family survive without you, and your income?
13. Are you ready to die right now?
14. How big is the officer you need to fight discounting the bullet proof vest he is wearing?
15. What does his eyes say about him? (Have you ever looked into a killers' eyes before? Do you recognize

what you are looking at)
16. Can you take his weapon, or weapons?
17. How many other officers are there? Will you fight them all.
18. Do you practice fighting skills, how frequently?
19. Have you been shot, or stabbed before?
20. How did you react to the wounding.
21. Have you ever seen a man killed in person, not television or internet.
22. What type of grip strength so you have? Can you keep the average man from pulling himself free of your grip.

The list above is not all inclusive it does not measure heart, or intensity. If you cannot answer yes to all the questions you probably won't make it through this fight depending on the officer. If you answer yes you still probably won't survive. But if it's my time to go, I just refuse to go begging another man to please let me live. If there are several officers no matter how good you are more than likely you will die. Your only real choice is whether you die fighting, or begging through a death gurgle. It's not fair, you did not choose this path but it is your path. Again if you do not meet the criteria listed above you don't even want to try starting the chain reaction that will ultimately end in your death. *I hope I have frightened you enough to make you never want to try this unless you have no other choice.*

The officer you are about to engage has practiced weapons retention, and combat techniques for hours and hours. If he has military training in the area and you are not an avid martial artist or mixed martial arts trained fighter your chances are little, to none for survival.

This is the absolute last thing I would ever recommend doing unless you already know the wolf is trying to take your life.

I told you the story earlier of a police officer having to confront a larger male. The officer told him that just the size difference between us gives me the right to use deadly force against you right now. Now get on the ground the young man complied and rightly so because he was less than 2 seconds from dying right there. The officer bragging about this was about 5'5" middle aged and out of shape. He hated everything, and that included me a black rookie. His first words to me once outside the earshot of the CO was you not going to make hit here so don't move to my city, I don't want you here. He was going through a nasty divorce, and he needed to hurt, or shoot someone bad. The aggression, and anger he had for his wife spilled out in self destructive ways, and in how he treated anyone he had control over.

Unprofessional, discourteous, corrupt and empowered.

 If this is the mentality of the officer you are fighting you will have to be very lucky to survive.

If you are in a situation where a police officer is in the process of punching you in the face don't panic. Use an old boxers move on him. He will probably be punching with his right hand because most people are right handed and that is his dominant hand. Which means he is more inclined to use it instinctively. It will also more than likely be his gun hand. Steady yourself and do not try and dodge it, or move away from him instead just as his fist is committed put your chin on your chest with your mouth shut tightly keep your tongue from between your teeth, and make sure that he punches you on the top of your forehead.

The forehead is one of the hardest bones in the human body. There is a high likelihood that the police officer will break his hand, his gun hand on your forehead. There is no guarantee but if he hurts it bad enough at minimum he will think twice about hitting you again.

Since the move you just executed will look like you were flinching prior to the blow he may not realize it was a calculated way of stopping his unlawful assault.

I have a great deal of reservations about sharing this type of information because someone may try and use it to hurt a good police officer. But most of the deaths, and beatings that I have detailed in this book, and the ones that appear across the internet are cops that do not deserve a badge, and all *the "good policemen" know them, know who they are and refuse to roust them out of the police departments across the nation so now they too must face the rising tide of animosity that is coming against police officers.*

I remember my cousin being beaten and thrown into a jail cell without any charges filed because he refused to sign tickets that were made up out of thin air. I remember the look in his eyes when he told me that a jailer opened his cell door and told him he could leave after about 4 hours of being locked in a cell alone. The officers beat his face into the hood of his car denting it in as a lesson to him to never POP (Piss Off the Police). He left with his face torn up and he had to pay to get his car out of the impound lot. No explanation, no apology just told to get out.

He was lucky they did not kill him. *If officers want respect, or empathy from the general population they will have to earn it. Too much has happened along the way, and too much has been lost in the way of professionalism for police officers to assume that the uniform alone does anything other than cover their nakedness. In other words the zero tolerance policy works both ways.*

The sad reality of it is that you are in a life and death struggle, kill, or be killed hesitation equals death. You may not have done anything to bring this on except get out of bed this morning.

Soft partially committed intent is poison, and it would be better to just keep your mouth shut and try not to further enrage this murdering jackal of a police officer than to put forth a half-hearted attempt to fight him off and have him screaming "stop trying to take my gun" "stop touching my gun" before shooting you in the chest 3 times. While your hands are covering you face for fear of being hit again.

You have to be strong, quick, have hard hand bones, be vicious, and have a merciless attitude, not an emotional fighter, willing to die, willing to kill, willing to survive, willing to go to prison, willing to lose everything, willing to take everything from him that he is willing to take from you. *If you are peaceful and he stomps, or tases you to death you lose everything anyway.*

You have to be 100 percent committed to doing whatever it takes to live without a nanosecond of hesitation even if you have to hold his hands and bite out his jugular, or windpipe, or head butt the bridge of his nose until it is as flat as a pancake, gouge his eyes or elbow him in the face, *your only objective is not to die at the hands of the wolf with a license to kill.*

The human head itself swivels and moves in every direction and it is difficult to hit with a fist. It is attached to shoulders, and a waist, and paired with two hands for blocking blows and now you see why it's so hard to count on hitting and effectively rendering unconscious a trained attacker. A quick internet search of street fights will show you that most punches to the head are ineffective for the unpracticed fighter. A grab and gouge is much more effective and has a higher probability of success.

Know for a fact if you engage the wolf, and he wins you will die, or you will wish you were dead. Biting is never expected as a move in a street fight. The front incisors are for shredding meat. I have seen a woman take down a burly man with her teeth dug into his shoulder. The violent way she shook her head, and his screams told the whole story she was a pit bulldog, and he did not want to hit her anymore. The sawing motion of her incisors cut deeply into him to the extent his plan to punch her became nonexistent and he began bargaining with her to let him go.

I know that the thought of having anyone else's blood in your mouth is not appealing but what if the only other choice you have is to be beaten to death. Do not take anything off the table that may help you survive.

Once engaged you do not want the officer's gun out of his holster. You will need above average grip strength in your hands which means you have been working them for years. Trying to keep a grown man's hand pinned in against your torso and not letting him reach his taser, or firearm holster will require more than desperation. You must keep his dominant hand pinned. You need to get him distracted and move his attention away from his gun. You have to use everything you have for a weapon in an effective manner. Step on his foot to keep him close, knee him in the groin, and or bite him in the neck or face. Use your legs to control the distance between you. Because he may fall down in an attempt to create distance to kill you. Anticipate this move and drop with him. You will not have the luxury of breaking your fall if it means letting go of his hands or wrists. Use your legs in the fashion of a grappler and dominate his position on the ground. Don't stop once engaged because in his mind someone has to die, and if he is winning it will be you. You may not choose to kill him if you win, and get him physically under control, or manage to choke him out. But if he wins the wolf will punch your ticket. Look for his gun side and prepare yourself to move to his gun side. It's usually the right side. If the officer is going to hit you there is a high probability that it will be with their dominant hand. You must be decisive and swift, blows that can disable an opponent require skills that only come through practice. Areas such as the neck just below the ear can easily be struck once an opponent has committed by extending their arm in a striking motion. The eye is easy to attack from a grappling position once the extended arm is secured.

You are not fighting for yourself you are fighting for your loved ones, your mom, your father, your sisters and brothers, your children born, or yet to be born and this animal who put you in this corner is only looking for another notch on his gun.

You have a right to live, and not die. You hopefully did not start this, or choose it. Hopefully you were courteous, and compliant and the officer has no justification to assault you, but now that you are in it do whatever it takes to

139

survive. If you have not practiced fighting start now, learn techniques. Get to a gym learn to take a punch, learn to punch effectively get stronger, get faster. *And most importantly pray that you never have to use it.*

Hopefully you will die in bed of old age, but if you are here now due to an abusive police officer it may be the only chance you may ever get to determine your fate.

If your life means anything to you, or any of your loved ones mean the world to you make up your mind now *what you are willing to do and prepare yourself for the moment that you and I pray never comes. The wolf in front of you has no conscious he will kill you and go to lunch without a second thought.* Know what you are going to do. Think through scenarios in your mind. Don't over estimate your skill, or underestimate the police officers' ability. If you have never been in a physical confrontation you need some serious real world enactments in the gym. It will tell you whether you are cut out for this kind of aggressiveness. Give others a chance to be honest with you about where you are as a fighter, and if you have enough skills.

If the officer attacks you unprovoked and grabs you with one hand, and you want to survive break the fingers on his gun hand quickly and ruthlessly break them however you have to do it. Most policemen are right handed so be practiced in your attack to the right hand. Fingers break quickly when bent sideways instead of straight back. If you can do so with one hand do it. If you have to use two hands to execute the move as quickly as possible because the wolf's other hand can be used to draw the taser, or pepper spray and controlling his hands is your only chance for survival. If he grabs you with his left hand on your left lapel area you should use your right hand to grab his weakest finger. Break any of the others you can get a quick grip on but usually the pinky finger is the most accessible. Viciously snap it sideways it will break. You may even hear it, or hear his painful response. Simultaneously his right hand will be going for his gun, taser, baton, or possible pepper spray. Again, you must control this hand. His first instinct will be to try and pull his hand away from you once his nerve signals his brain that his hand has been injured.

Be prepared but do not count on the officer balling up in agony. If he is in a rage he may not even feel it. Not everyone reacts to pain immediately. But no matter what your grip on the wolf's hand it cannot be released. You lose this grip and you probably lose your life. Again' you need his to stay close to him don't let him pull away from you, or you are dead. If you can pull him into your body by his hands, or move your feet so that you stay as close to him as possible this is the optimum position. Learning to grapple will prepare you. Expect to be kneed in the groin area. You want to be close enough to smell his breath. Use the hardest bone in your body to head butt him in the nose, not the forehead or the eye you need to go completely through his nose with your forehead. If he attempts to head butt you dodge to his gun side and attack his throat with your teeth. It will distract him from his weapons.

Thoughts of peaceful resolution are long gone sell out to the moment, or perish. Hopefully you are processing, and ready for the next step of biting deeply into his neck, not his face his neck. If you have to start at his face until he is distracted enough to yield his neck by pulling away his head from your teeth then use it. He will instinctively pull his face away from your mouth let him win this it will expose his neck. You will now enter a much more intense struggle as the officers rage, and desperation take over their emotions and he attempts with even more desperation to reach his weapons. However' as you aggressively make a sawing motion with your teeth into his skin like that of a dog shaking its prey. The wolfs hands will began to pull away from his weapons and attempt to free your teeth from his throat.

If you are on the ground use your legs to keep his legs apart as I said before mixed martial arts training on ground and pound will demonstrate and help you become proficient with the technique. By placing your legs between his and keeping them apart you can control his leverage and keep him pinned, as well as keep him from rolling over. All these are dependent on you having practiced, and practiced, and practiced until it becomes second nature for you. There will be blood, metallic tasting blood in your mouth and on your clothes and face. Once you hit an artery on either side of his neck you will know.

You were a few moments from going to jail severely beaten if you were lucky, or the hospital, or the morgue if you were unlucky. You were at the mercy of a wolf.

Nothing has changed you are still possibly a guilty verdict away from lethal injection. The last ditch efforts of dying people are surprising be prepared for the last few moments they may be the most violent. ***Don't lose your intensity because you think you are winning.***

Even if you win there will be serious consequences but you will be alive to face them. Or you could just let the officer kill you, and then go to lunch with his buddies, and brag about the death gurgle you made as the light faded from your eyes. Or maybe he will high five your dead body Like officer Mark Tiller is accused of doing to a teenager he shot in the back. You decide before you ever get forced into the situation.

I choose this gruesome method of talking you through such a confrontation as a means of dissuading you from even trying it except under the most dire of circumstances. I did not advise you to throw strikes to the wolf's head because most people think that they are better than they actually are with it comes to striking. And the chances of knocking out the wolf are minimal for most people.
I know that most people do not know how to fight well at all, and they definitely do not have what it takes to out fight a police officer with access to any assortment of training and weapons at his disposal. If you have not learned to punch with maximum effectiveness in close combat I can't teach you that through a book. Nor can I teach you to apply a choke hold from the front, or side for an armed officer while lying on his gun hand with your body weight. But most people have incisors and in a desperate life and death struggle you use what you have. Elbows, head butts, knees etc....

Do not charge the officer, you won't make it. The physical engagement must be initiated by him in order to for the finger break technique to work. If you can incapacitate him badly enough you may not have to kill him.

If the officer is swinging at you then you may have to try and clinch or grab him to get close enough to use the techniques I just related. No fight is a sure thing but if it's your only choice I want you to survive.

If the officer takes out a baton do not try and block it with your hands allow it to glace off your forearm and into your body. Once there lock it in with your arm. If you are quick enough to get inside his swing and take most of the momentum out of his swing then do so. When he hits you it is going to hurt so be prepared to function through the pain. The only way to extract the baton is to pull it straight back. At that time you can grab the hand and control it. Most police are as inadequate at fighting off their backs as is the average American. If you practice these moves over and over you may have a 35 to 45 percent survival rate they are not easy. If you do nothing your life can end right there at the discretion of the wolf with a badge. You can always crawl into a ball and cover your face and head with your arms and end up like the picture below

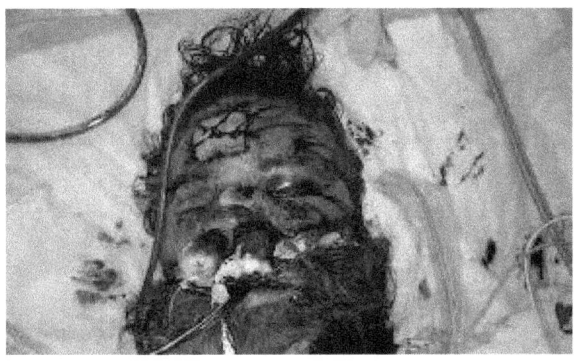

Do you think that at some point the officers involved in beating this mentally ill man who was crying for his daddy with each blow could have stopped before he died? At some point he was done fighting or resisting but the wolves in uniforms insisted on him dying that day. That's right he did not make it. He died calling for his dad to save him like the little 12 year old girl screaming for her dad as she was beaten into a hospital bed by 3 grown men with badges.

Maybe this child was too much to handle and needed to be shot in face with a taser by police officers while his hands were cuffed behind him.

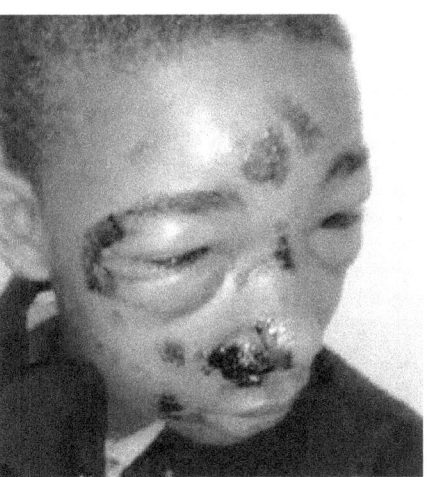

The officer who did it said the child was running away from him and he had no choice but to shoot the boy in the face as he ran AWAY from him. This is why we must fight and win. The wolf has no hesitation in destroying anyone in his bloody path.

DARK HORIZONS

The news around the country is rife with reports of police officers being ambushed and killed by vigilante extremists who are feeding off the rising tide of protest with the common theme that "Black Lives Matter". This movement is continuing to gain momentum and is probably not near its peak. The problem is that on its fringes lurk those who openly call for, and celebrate the murder of police officers as a way of obtaining justice for the many documented, and undocumented atrocities committed by police officers against citizens in this country on a daily basis. Attacks like the one carried out against the Dallas Police Department with an armored van can spark responses such as copy cat crimes as well as having the effect of driving officers into a shoot first and ask questions later us against them mindset.

Earlier I said something to the effect that violence becomes the voice of the voiceless. In almost every war torn country, or terror driven conflict one side feels that they are not being heard or represented as did the founding fathers of this country. Which lead to the American revolution. Likewise certain segments of our population have for generations been unheard and unrepresented when they cried out for justice with claims of being mistreated by the police who swore an oath to protect them.

Now we face on a day to day basis police officers who are leaving the station to go on duty with the mindset of going to war for their own survival instead of going on duty to protect and serve the citizens of their community. Officers like Daniel Holtzclaw who was convicted of raping over 10 women under the color of the badge completely remove most public sympathy and cause a back lash of ill feelings and negative responses toward all uniformed police officers.

The news media will try and twist it into a racial issue but as documented in this book it is not a completely racial issue. That is a ploy to try and keep Americans asleep and uninformed. For the most part it is an abuse of powers issue, working in tandem with a biased courts issue, which is compounded by racially motivated legislation on the part of congress. Case in point was the not too recently overturned legislation that called for strict sentencing guidelines for crack cocaine but not for cocaine itself. One drug popular in one community, while another dominated a different segment of society.

Another case in point would be the legislation that was passed to prosecute drug dealers for murder if one of their customers overdosed. This was done after a myriad of overdoses in well-heeled communities offended certain people. At that point the witch hunt was on to prosecute the drug users pushers for their deaths. This was made ever so clear when Carrol O'Connor suffered the loss of his son to an overdose who was a known drug addict and had made statements to the effect that he could not survive another rehab attempt. But no congressperson thought to pursue any drug dealers in the poorer communities for murder when the less well off died from overdoses.

It was not long ago that Americans were pointing high powered rifles at federal officers in an attempt to protect a land owner form having their land seized by a corrupt government at the Bundy Ranch in Nevada. No nationwide move was made against them for trying to fight for land rights.

Statistically while white males make up 33% of the population they make up 66% of law enforcement and 95% of prosecutors, and 65% of elected officials. 14% of Americans are black but prison populations of black men, and women in America hover near 50% for both sexes.

It becomes undeniable that there has been a systemic targeting of blacks in this country. It now is also undeniable that so to are white Americans finding themselves under the boot heels of the wolves with badges. large numbers of Americans are fed up and a few are willing do what Americans forefathers did and began to lash out at the representatives of this system in ways that may not be popular with the rest of the country. A survey of the American revolutionary war will revealed that most Americans did not want to fight a war with Great Britain in fact George Washington was in the minority on this issue but his conscious as a man demanded that he stand up.

I challenge anyone on the other side of this opinion to lose their loved ones by hanging, rape, torture, and humiliation from generation to generation and not come to this same place of defiance, and determination to stop at all cost the system that would kill, imprison, and demoralize your children, and the sons of your sons, and the daughters of your daughters. A system that herds them into cages, and brands them for life as a way of controlling and subjugating them generationally.

Every British soldier that died during the American Revolution had family, friends and loved ones who missed him dearly, and undoubtedly cried at his loss. But violence becomes the voice of the voiceless. Every oppressor attempts to justify their actions by the manipulation of the masses through the media and this includes

America. I cannot help but feel pain and sympathy for every police officer who has lost their lives to violence. It is the same pain I feel for the lives that have been taken by police officers who are never bought to proper justice. The glaring difference is that every police officer knows an officer that should not be wearing a badge but has refused to address it and so the 15% of bad apples in the basket do spoil the entire basket. When 12 year olds are killed while playing with toy pistols in the park and young fathers are gunned down in Walmart for holding a BB gun in less than 1 second there is no room for misinterpretation, when an officer hi fives the dead bodies of unarmed teens who have just been shot there is no room for misinterpretation. The message is clear to every American citizen who cares enough to just look at the evidence.

Peruse the websites below and see for yourself the devastation that draws no sympathy or action for the fallen men, and women of the subjugated communities of our America. And ask yourselves

http://gawker.com/unarmed-people-of-color-killed-by-police-1999-2014-1666672349

http://www.rolereboot.org/culture-and-politics/details/2014-08-black-unarmed-women-girls-without-weapons-killed-law-enforcement/

CONCLUSION

Across America we find daily that as more, and more incidents of police abuses, and corruption come to light it brings about less, and less trust for the badge. Seemingly rather than the agencies sworn to protect us attempting a new approach to restore their standing with the American citizens they have instead chosen to ratchet up the abuses, and even push to silence the voices that call for them to be accountable.

A few officers are attempting to sound off about abuses but those few find themselves ostracized, marginalized and often fired for attempting to hold their peers accountable. There are no easy answers but there are some answers that cannot be denied, or delayed. Every policeman knows who the bad officers are. These wolves with a license to kill citizens have to be stopped. There is no way around it. They don't need remedial training they need new careers in some other capacity other than carrying a gun.

Americans everywhere need to see this problem for what it is and not allow complacency or media bias to sway them from the truth. The old euphemism about not breaking the law and then not having to fear the police has been proven wrong. We all see instances of innocent citizens of every persuasion being harassed, abused, and killed coming to light daily. We are forced to acknowledge that a guitar string can only be tightened so much before the inevitable happens.

I hope to see Americans rise up and hold accountable those who are in power and to continue to hold them accountable ***until the tide turns for every citizen and we can again look at a policeman and tell our children without fear that "if you are in trouble you can tell a policeman and he will help you".*** One can hope but one can also work for an expected outcome.

The judicial branch with all its smoke, and mirrors has contributed to the current situation in our country as well. It seems to turn a blind eye to innocent citizens being railroaded into private prisons for the sake of making money off the backs of the poorest of our citizens, and generationally dooming the next generation to the lives of dark statistics.

Review these cases and then you decide if American citizens can afford to do nothing to bring the change so desperately needed.

Cops Shoot Unarmed Teen in the Back then High-Five his .
thefreethoughtproject.com/witness-officers-plant-evidence-high-teens-bo...
Aug 15, 2015 - Zach-Hammond-witness-high-five-dead-body ... a witness has come forward who reportedly saw officers high-fiving Hammond's corpse after ...

http://thefreethoughtproject.com/61-year-old-man-violently-attacked-police-arrested-singing-beach-boys-song/

https://www.facebook.com/OutFrontCNN/videos/vb.102938906478343/665924283513133/?type=2&theater

http://6abc.com/news/cop-indicted-after-video-shows-suspect-kicked-in-head/703334/
Man complying with get down on the ground order and is kicked unconscious by officer

http://countercurrentnews.com/2015/02/philly-cops-charged/
cops chase and beat man fleeing on scooter

http://thefreethoughtproject.com/man-brandishes-gun-ward-intruders-cops-show-shoot-2-seconds/
Police shoot man who called for help with home invasion.

http://atlantablackstar.com/2015/05/11/the-emotion-on-this-mans-face-after-seeing-the-video-of-police-beating-him-for-the-first-time-is-heart-wrenching/
Man sees himself beaten by LAPD for first time. His attorney says other police on the scene never tried to him

http://thefreethoughtproject.com/woman-shot-police-defending-estranged-husband-broke-home-threatened-gun

http://thefreethoughtproject.com/man-calls-cops-report-vandals-home-show-kill/
man calls police and tells them vandals are outside and he has gun. Police show up and shoot him.

http://thefreethoughtproject.com/isolated-incident-caught-video-police-beating-handcuffed-man/
police beat handcuffed prisoner

http://alternativemediasyndicate.com/2015/01/16/cops-shoot-man-who-had-toy-gun-7-times-in-the-back/
police shoot man with pellet gun 7 times after he told then that he had it and it was not loaded

http://thefreethoughtproject.com/breaking-video-finally-released-cops-shooting-man-toy-gun-wal-mart/open carry no law violated, bb gun in Walmart shot down from behind no warning

http://thefreethoughtproject.com/video-refutes-cops-claim-fearing-life-shot-unarmed-boy-syndrome/
teen shot trying to flee police in mom's minivan

http://thefreethoughtproject.com/cop-guilty-caught-video-stomping-subdued-mans-face/
police kick and stomp tased and subdued man in head

http://countercurrentnews.com/2014/12/cop-man-recording-arrest-with-cellphone/
man gets choked and body slammed for legally recording arrest.

http://www.cnn.com/2014/09/25/justice/south-carolina-trooper-shooting/.